Hey ya'll!
How are ya'll doing
on this AMAZING day?
I am doing good. I am blessed.
I am highly favored in the lord
and even when I think that I am not
I am not I still am...

That's Good Right There!

EASY-DELICIOUS-SOULFUL MEALS

KELLEY HARRIS

INTRODUCTION

Welcome to My Kitchen!
Hello, food lovers! I'm Kellz, the heart and soul behind ItsMeKellz. Cooking has always been my passion, and I'm thrilled to share my culinary journey with you through this cookbook. Whether you're a seasoned chef or just starting out, my goal is to make cooking fun, accessible, and delicious for everyone.

A Journey of Flavors
From my earliest memories, the kitchen has been a place of joy, creativity, and connection. Growing up, I was inspired by the rich, diverse flavors of my family's cooking. This cookbook is a celebration of those flavors, infused with my own twists and innovations. Each recipe is crafted with love and designed to bring people together around the table.

What You'll Find Inside
In this cookbook, you'll discover a variety of recipes that cater to all tastes and occasions. From quick and easy weeknight dinners to indulgent desserts, there's something for everyone. I've included tips and tricks to help you master each dish, along with personal anecdotes that make each recipe special.

Let's Cook Together
Cooking is more than just preparing food; it's about creating memories and sharing experiences. I encourage you to experiment with these recipes, make them your own, and most importantly, have fun in the kitchen. Remember, the best meals are made with love and shared with those we care about.
Thank you for joining me on this culinary adventure. Let's get cooking!
Warmest regards,
Kellz

Prayer

First and foremost, I express my gratitude to my Heavenly Father for all the blessings bestowed upon me. Without Your constant presence by my side, Lord, where would I be today? Thank you for the wonderful gifts, the supportive people around me, and the platform to share them. Your peace in my heart is truly appreciated, as well as the opportunity to speak about Your amazing deeds. I am filled with gratitude for the avenue to give back and serve Your purpose. My thanks know no bounds, as I appreciate Your presence every single day. I vow to follow Your teachings faithfully in all my endeavors. You are the ultimate authority, and though life on earth is temporary, I find solace in knowing that I will dwell with You eternally in Your kingdom. Amen.

Kelley Harris

MEET KELLZ

Hey everyone, I'm Kellz, and a warm welcome to my kitchen! Before we dive into cooking, let me share a bit about myself. I'm Kelley Harris, the creative force behind "It's Me Kellz." My culinary background is a blend of traditional and modern techniques. I consider myself a cook rather than a chef, drawing inspiration from family recipes passed down through generations and dishes I've come to adore. My culinary journey focuses on replicating recipes, known as "copycat cooking," to bring restaurant-quality meals to home kitchens. From Southern favorites like fried chicken and banana pudding to contemporary delights such as Philly cheese steak egg rolls and citrus grilled salmon, my repertoire is diverse. On social media, I share cooking tutorials, revealing the step-by-step process behind these mouthwatering dishes. Beyond just cooking, my videos aim to share a piece of my culinary heritage and invite viewers into my kitchen. By simplifying complex recipes, I've cultivated a community of food enthusiasts who appreciate my down-to-earth approach. Whether you're a seasoned chef or a novice, I hope my recipes and tips spark creativity in your kitchen. Since childhood, my dream was to follow in my mom's footsteps and become a cook. She instilled in me the belief that people eat with their eyes first, emphasizing the importance of presentation and cooking with love. As an adult, I pursued my passion, becoming a food blogger and launching my cooking channel. Even today, when I cook, I feel my mom's presence in the kitchen, her legacy living on through my culinary creations. So I welcome you now let's get to cooking.

RECIPES

From My Family To Yours

A heartfelt thank you to all my followers for their continuous support in my culinary adventures. Your kind words, thoughtful gifts, and love have truly touched my heart. I am deeply grateful to each and every one of you for standing by me. These roses serve as a symbol of my appreciation, representing the friendship and happiness you bring into my life. Your warmth and affection always brighten my days. Thank you for accompanying me on this journey. May you all be blessed abundantly.

TABLE OF CONTENTS

KITCHEN

Conversion & Cooking Chart

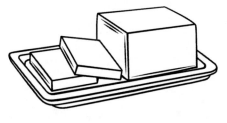

1 stick
1/2 cup
1/4 lb

Spoons

1 Tbsp
3 Tsp
1/2 oz
15 ml

Dash / Pinch

1/16 tsp   1/8 tsp

CUPS	OUNCES	TABLESPOONS	TEASPOONS
1	8	16	48
3/4	6	12	36
2/3	5	11	32
1/2	4	8	24
1/3	3	5	16
1/4	2	4	12

2 cups = 1 pint
2 Pints = 1 Quart
4 quarts = 1 gallon

Kitchen
CONVERSIONS

1 gallon

1 Gallon
4 Quarts
8 Pints
16 Cups
128 Ounces
38 Liters

1 quart

1 Quart
2 Pints
4 Cups
32 Ounces
45 Liters

1 pint

1 Pint
2 Cups
16 Ounces
481 ML

1 cup

4 tbsp
12 tsp
2 fl oz
60 ml

1/ 4 cup

16 tbsp
8 fl oz
240 ml

10

KITCHEN
Conversion & Cooking Chart

DRY MEASURMENTS

1/2 oz	1 tbsp	1/6 c	15 g	-------
1 oz	2 tbsp	1/8 c	28 g	-------
2 oz	4 tbsp	1/4 c	57 g	-------
3 oz	6 tbsp	1/3 c	85 g	-------
4 oz	8 tbsp	1/2 c	115 g	1/4 lb
8 oz	16 tbsp	1 c	227 g	1/2 lb
12 oz	24 tbsp	1 1/2 c	340 g	3/4 lb
16 oz	32 tbsp	2 c	455 g	1 lb

LIQUID MEASURMENT

1 oz	6 tsp	2 tbsp	30 ml	1/8 c	-------	-------
2 oz	12 tsp	4 tbsp	60 ml	1/4 c	-------	-------
2 2/3 oz	16 tsp	5 tbsp	80 ml	1/3 c	-------	-------
4 oz	24 tsp	8 tbsp	120 ml	1/2 c	-------	-------
5 1/3 oz	32 tsp	11 tbsp	160 ml	2/3 c	-------	-------
6 oz	26 tsp	12 tbsp	177 ml	3/4 c	-------	-------
8 oz	48 tsp	16 tbsp	240 ml	1 c	1/2 pt	1/4 qt
16 oz	96 tsp	32 tbsp	470 ml	2 c	1 pt	1/2 qt
32 oz	192 tsp	64 tbsp	95 ml	4 c	2 pt	1 qt

KITCHEN

Conversion & Cooking Chart

OVEN TEMPERATURES

 225 250 275 300 325 350 375 400 425 450 475 500

 110 120 140 150 170 180 190 200 220 230 240 260

EGG TIMERS

Soft - 5 min
Medium - 7 minutes
Hard - 9 minutes

HERBS

1 tsp dried = 1 tbsp fresh

Kellz Tips and Techniques

1 Read the Recipe First: Before you start cooking, read through the entire recipe. This helps you understand the steps and ensures you have all the necessary ingredients and tools.

2 Prep Ingredients Ahead of Time: Measure and prepare all your ingredients before you start cooking. This is called "mise en place" and it makes the cooking process smoother and more enjoyable.

3 Use Fresh Ingredients: Fresh ingredients often have better flavor and nutritional value. Whenever possible, use fresh herbs, vegetables, and meats.

4 Season as You Go: Don't wait until the end to season your food. Add salt, pepper, and other seasonings at different stages of cooking to build layers of flavor.

5 Taste and Adjust: Always taste your food as you cook. This allows you to adjust the seasoning and make sure the flavors are balanced.

6 Keep Your Knives Sharp: A sharp knife is safer and more efficient than a dull one. Regularly sharpen your knives to make chopping and slicing easier.

7 Don't Overcrowd the Pan: When sautéing or frying, give your ingredients enough space. Overcrowding the pan can cause food to steam rather than brown.

8 Let Meat Rest: After cooking meat, let it rest for a few minutes before cutting into it. This helps the juices redistribute, making the meat more tender and flavorful.

9 Use a Thermometer: For perfectly cooked meat, use a meat thermometer to check the internal temperature. This ensures your meat is cooked to the right doneness without being overcooked.

10 Clean as You Go: Keep your workspace tidy by cleaning up as you cook. This makes the process more enjoyable and less overwhelming at the end.

Happy cooking!

APPETIZERS

BANG BANG SHRIMP

 Prep Time 15 Minutes

 Cooking Time 2 to 3 Minutes

Temp: 350 degrees

INGREDIENTS

1 lb. shrimp
peeled and deveined.
1 teaspoon seafood creole
1 teaspoon garlic powder
1 teaspoon paprika
THE MARINADE
½ cup sour cream
¼ cup heavy cream
1/4 cup milk
1 teaspoon paprika
1 teaspoon garlic powder
THE DREDGE/DRY MIX
2 cups flour
1 cup cornstarch
1 tablespoon seafood creole
1 teaspoon garlic powder
1 teaspoon paprika
THE SAUCE
½ cup mayonnaise
1 teaspoon sriracha
¼ cup Thai sweet chili sauce
1 teaspoon garlic powder
1 teaspoon soy sauce

DIRECTIONS 4

TO PREPARE THESE MOUTHWATERING BANG BANG SHRIMP, START BY COMBINING THE SHRIMP, CREOLE SEASONING, GARLIC POWDER, AND PAPRIKA IN A LARGE BOWL. IN A SEPARATE BOWL, MIX TOGETHER THE SOUR CREAM, HEAVY CREAM, MILK, PAPRIKA, AND GARLIC POWDER UNTIL WELL BLENDED. POUR THE MILK MIXTURE OVER THE SHRIMP AND STIR TO COMBINE, THEN SET IT ASIDE WHILE YOU PREPARE THE DRY BATTER.

IN ANOTHER LARGE BOWL, MIX THE FLOUR, CORNSTARCH, SEAFOOD CREOLE SEASONING, AND GARLIC POWDER THOROUGHLY. IN A LARGE POT OR DEEP FRYER, HEAT THE OIL TO 350 DEGREES. ONCE THE OIL REACHES THE RIGHT TEMPERATURE, DREDGE THE SHRIMP IN THE DRY MIXTURE AND CAREFULLY PLACE EACH ONE INTO THE FRYER. COOK FOR 2 TO 3 MINUTES, THEN REMOVE THE SHRIMP TO A DRAINING RACK TO KEEP THEM CRISPY.

NEXT, PREPARE THE BANG BANG SAUCE. IN A SMALL BOWL, COMBINE THE MAYONNAISE, SRIRACHA, SWEET CHILI SAUCE, GARLIC POWDER, AND SOY SAUCE, MIXING WELL. TRANSFER THE COOKED SHRIMP TO A LARGE BOWL, POUR THE BANG BANG SAUCE OVER THE TOP, AND TOSS TO ENSURE EACH PIECE IS WELL COATED. SERVE ON A PLATE AND ENJOY!

CORN NUGGETS

 Prep Time 10 minutes

 Cooking Time
15 Minutes

INGREDIENTS

4

Corn Nuggets

1 cup all-purpose flour

(I use White Lilly)

¼ cup yellow corn meal

(I use Martha White Self-

Rising)

1 ½ teaspoon baking

powder

2 tablespoons sugar

1 teaspoon salt

¼ teaspoon cayenne

pepper

2 cups corn(Fresh corn is

sweeter)

1 egg

½ cup milk

DIRECTIONS

TO MAKE DELICIOUS CORN NUGGETS, START BY MIXING FLOUR, CORN MEAL, SUGAR, SALT, AND BAKING POWDER IN A MEDIUM BOWL. ONCE COMBINED, ADD IN THE WET INGREDIENTS - EGGS, CORN MILK, AND A DASH OF CAYENNE PEPPER. HEAT OIL TO 350 DEGREES AND USE A SMALL SCOOP TO ADD THE BATTER INTO THE HOT OIL. LET THE NUGGETS COOK FOR 3 TO 4 MINUTES UNTIL THEY ARE GOLDEN BROWN. ONCE COOKED, REMOVE THEM TO A PAPER TOWEL TO DRAIN. FOR AN EXTRA TOUCH OF SWEETNESS, DRIZZLE SOME RAW HONEY ON THEM WHILE THEY ARE STILL HOT. ENJOY THESE TASTY TREATS!

DEEP FRIED ZUCCHINI

 Prep Time 15 Minutes

 Cooking Time 10 Minutes

Temp: 325 degrees

INGREDIENTS

Deep Fried Zucchini

2 Zucchinis sliced into ¼ inch circles

2 eggs

¼ cup milk

1 cup flour

1 teaspoon creole seasoning

1 teaspoon onion powder

1 teaspoon garlic powder

1 teaspoon pepper

2 cups Italian panko breadcrumbs

Oil for frying

DIRECTIONS 4

TO PREPARE THESE DELICIOUS DEEP-FRIED ZUCCHINIS, BEGIN BY ESTABLISHING A DREDGING STATION. IN A MEDIUM BOWL, COMBINE EGGS AND MILK, THEN SET IT ASIDE. IN ANOTHER BOWL, MIX TOGETHER FLOUR, CREOLE SEASONING, ONION POWDER, GARLIC POWDER, AND PEPPER, AND THEN SET IT ASIDE AS WELL. IN A SEPARATE BOWL, PLACE YOUR BREADCRUMBS. ARRANGE ALL THESE ITEMS SIDE BY SIDE TO CREATE YOUR DREDGING STATION.

NOW, LET'S START THE DREDGING PROCESS. FIRST, DIP EACH ZUCCHINI SLICE IN THE FLOUR MIXTURE, THEN IN THE EGG MIXTURE, AND FINALLY COAT IT WITH BREADCRUMBS BEFORE TRANSFERRING IT TO A BAKING SHEET. REPEAT THIS UNTIL ALL THE ZUCCHINIS ARE BREADED, THEN SET THEM ASIDE.

IN A LARGE SKILLET, ADD OIL AND PREHEAT IT TO 325 DEGREES. BEGIN ADDING YOUR BREADED ZUCCHINIS TO THE HOT OIL. FRY THEM FOR ABOUT TWO TO THREE MINUTES ON EACH SIDE, OR UNTIL THEY TURN GOLDEN BROWN AND CRISPY. ONCE COOKED, REMOVE THEM FROM THE OIL AND PLACE THEM ON A DRAINING RACK TO KEEP THEM CRISPY. CONTINUE THIS PROCESS UNTIL ALL YOUR ZUCCHINIS ARE FRIED. SERVE WITH MARINARA SAUCE AND ENJOY!

JALAPENO HUSHPUPPIES

 Prep Time 15 Minutes

 Cooking Time 5 Minutes

Temp: 325 degrees

INGREDIENTS

1 cup self-rising corn meal

1/2 cup flour

2 tablespoons chopped jalapenos

1/2 cup cream corn

1 egg

1/4 cup water

oil for frying

DIRECTIONS 6

TO PREPARE THESE TASTY JALAPEÑO HUSHPUPPIES, START BY MIXING CORNMEAL, FLOUR, ONIONS, JALAPEÑOS, AND CORN IN A MEDIUM BOWL UNTIL WELL COMBINED. LET THE MIXTURE REST FOR AROUND 10 MINUTES. IN A LARGE POT, HEAT OIL TO 325 DEGREES. ONCE THE OIL IS HOT, USE A SCOOP TO DROP THE MIXTURE INTO THE OIL AND FRY FOR ABOUT 5 MINUTES OR UNTIL THEY TURN GOLDEN BROWN. MOVE THEM TO A DRAINING RACK TO ELIMINATE ANY EXCESS OIL. FINALLY, PAIR THEM WITH SOME SWEET CHILI SAUCE AND ENJOY!

LEMON PEPPER WINGS

 Prep Time 15 Minutes

 Cooking Time 25 Minutes

INGREDIENTS

1 ½ pound chicken wings
1 tablespoon garlic powder
1 tablespoon onion powder
1 tablespoon creole seasoning
Lemon Pepper Sauce
1 cup butter (melted)
¼ cup fresh squeezed lemon juice
1 teaspoon onion powder
1 teaspoon garlic powder
2 tablespoons lemon pepper
seasoning parsley for garnish
Oil used: Canola oil
Oil Temp: 375 degrees Fahrenheit
Cooking Time 25 minutes

DIRECTIONS 4

PREHEAT THE OIL TO 375 DEGREES FAHRENHEIT. IN A LARGE BOWL, MIX THE CHICKEN WINGS WITH GARLIC POWDER, ONION POWDER, AND CREOLE SEASONING. NEXT, TRANSFER THE SEASONED WINGS TO A DEEP FRYER AND COOK THEM FOR 25 MINUTES. WHILE THE WINGS FRY, PREPARE THE LEMON PEPPER SAUCE. IN A MICROWAVE-SAFE BOWL, MELT THE BUTTER, THEN STIR IN THE LEMON JUICE, ONION POWDER, GARLIC POWDER, AND LEMON PEPPER SEASONING UNTIL WELL COMBINED. SET THIS MIXTURE ASIDE. ONCE THE WINGS ARE COOKED, TAKE THEM OUT OF THE FRYER AND PLACE THEM IN A BOWL. POUR THE LEMON PEPPER SAUCE OVER THE WINGS AND TOSS TO ENSURE THEY ARE EVENLY COATED. SERVE THE WINGS ON A PLATTER WITH YOUR FAVORITE DIPPING SAUCE. DRIZZLE ANY LEFTOVER LEMON PEPPER SAUCE OVER THE WINGS, GARNISH WITH PARSLEY, AND ENJOY!

ONION RINGS

 Prep Time 15 Minutes

 Cooking Time 25 Minutes

Temp: 350 degrees

INGREDIENTS

1 large Vidalia onion
(cut into slices)
1 cup all purpose flour
1/2 cup corn starch
1 teaspoon onion powder
1 teaspoon garlic powder
1 tablespoons Creole seasoning
1 1/2 cups sparking water, club
soda or beer if you like.
(If the batter is too thick add more
it should look like pancake batter)
2 cups panko bread crumbs
1 teaspoon creole seasoning
salt & pepper to taste
THE HONEY MUSTARD
1/2 cup mustard
1 teaspoon mayonnaise
1 tablespoon honey
1 tablespoon brown-sugar

DIRECTIONS 4

TO PREPARE THESE SCRUMPTIOUS ONION RINGS, BEGIN BY SLICING YOUR ONIONS INTO ½ INCH RINGS. IN A LARGE BOWL, COMBINE ALL-PURPOSE FLOUR, CORNSTARCH, ONION POWDER, GARLIC POWDER, AND CREOLE SEASONING. NEXT, POUR IN THE SPARKLING WATER, CLUB SODA, OR BEER, AND MIX UNTIL THE BATTER REACHES A CONSISTENCY SIMILAR TO PANCAKE BATTER. SET THIS MIXTURE ASIDE WHILE YOU CREATE THE DRY COATING. IN A SEPARATE MEDIUM BOWL, MIX BREADCRUMBS, ADDITIONAL CREOLE SEASONING, SALT, AND PEPPER THOROUGHLY.

NOW, TAKE EACH ONION RING, DIP IT INTO THE WET MIXTURE, THEN COAT IT IN THE DRY MIXTURE, AND PLACE IT ON A BAKING SHEET. REPEAT THIS PROCESS UNTIL ALL THE RINGS ARE PREPARED. ONCE FINISHED, HEAT OIL TO 350° IN A LARGE POT OR DEEP FRYER. WHEN THE OIL IS HOT, CAREFULLY ADD THE ONION RINGS, ENSURING THEY HAVE ENOUGH SPACE TO AVOID STICKING TOGETHER. FRY THE RINGS FOR ABOUT TWO TO THREE MINUTES, OR UNTIL THEY TURN GOLDEN BROWN. REMOVE THEM AND PLACE THEM ON A DRAINING RACK TO MAINTAIN THEIR CRISPINESS.

NOW, LET'S WHIP UP A DELIGHTFUL HONEY MUSTARD SAUCE. IN A SMALL BOWL, MIX TOGETHER MUSTARD, MAYONNAISE, HONEY, AND BROWN SUGAR. FINALLY, SERVE YOUR ONION RINGS ON A PLATE ALONGSIDE THIS TASTY HONEY MUSTARD DIPPING SAUCE, AND ENJOY!

SWEET HEAT RIBS

 Prep Time 15 Minutes

 Cooking Time 1 Hour 30 Minutes

INGREDIENTS

1 slab of baby back ribs
1/3 cup rice or apple cider vinegar
2 tablespoons yellow mustard
1 teaspoon sweet heat seasoning
1 teaspoon smokey rub seasoning
1 teaspoon Kinder s Wood Fire Garlic seasoning
1 teaspoon roasted garlic powder
Sweet Heat Sauce
1/2 cup melted butter
1 teaspoon sweet heat seasoning
1 teaspoon woodfire garlic (Kinders)
1 teaspoon smoky rub
2 tablespoons masterpiece teriyaki sauce
2 tablespoons raw honey
2 tablespoons hot sauce
1 tablespoon brown sugar

DIRECTIONS 4

TO PREPARE THE SWEET HEAT RIBS START BY REMOVING THE MEMBRANE FROM THE REAR OF THE RIBS. SUBSEQUENTLY, TRIM EXCESS FAT AND SEGMENT THE RIBS INTO INDIVIDUAL PORTIONS. PLACE THEM IN A BOWL, ADD RICE VINEGAR, AND MARINATE FOR 30 MINUTES BEFORE DISCARDING THE VINEGAR. NEXT, INCORPORATE MUSTARD, SWEET HEAT, KINDER'S WOODFIRE GARLIC, SMOKEY RUB, AND ROASTED GARLIC, ENSURING A THOROUGH MIXTURE. POSITION THE RIBS ON A BAKING SHEET AND PLACE IN A PREHEATED OVEN AT 375 DEGREES FOR 11/2 HOURS OR UNTIL TENDER. CONCURRENTLY, PREPARE THE SAUCE BY COMBINING BUTTER, SWEET HEAT, WOODFIRE GARLIC, SMOKEY RUB, TERIYAKI SAUCE, HONEY, HOT SAUCE, AND SUGAR IN A SMALL BOWL. UPON COMPLETION OF THE RIBS' COOKING TIME, APPLY THE SWEET HEAT SAUCE AND RETURN TO THE OVEN FOR AN ADDITIONAL 10 MINUTES. REMOVE, LET REST FOR 10 MINUTES, AND SERVE WITH ADDITIONAL SAUCE IF DESIRED. NOTE: THIS RECIPE MAY REQUIRE MODIFICATIONS FOR INDIVIDUALS WITH DIETARY RESTRICTIONS OR FOOD ALLERGIES, SO PLEASE REVIEW INGREDIENTS CAREFULLY AND MAKE NECESSARY SUBSTITUTIONS.

22

BREADS

CRACKLING HO CAKES

 Prep Time 15 Minutes

 Cooking Time 25 Minutes

INGREDIENTS

2 cups self-rising corn meal
¼ cup sugar
1 egg
1 cup pork cracklings
3/4 cup milk
¾ cup water
canola oil for cooking

DIRECTIONS 4

TO CREATE A DELICIOUS BATCH OF TRADITIONAL SOUTHERN CRACKLING HO CAKES, FOLLOW THESE SIMPLE STEPS. IN A MEDIUM BOWL, COMBINE THE SELF-RISING CORNMEAL, SUGAR, EGG, CRACKLINGS, MILK, AND WATER, AND MIX EVERYTHING TOGETHER UNTIL WELL COMBINED. HEAT A MEDIUM SKILLET OVER MEDIUM HEAT AND ADD IN THE CANOLA OIL. ONCE THE OIL IS HOT, SPOON OUT THE BATTER INTO THE PAN TO MAKE SMALL CAKES. COOK FOR 2 TO 3 MINUTES ON ONE SIDE, OR UNTIL THE CAKES ARE A GOLDEN-BROWN COLOR. THEN, FLIP THEM OVER AND CONTINUE COOKING FOR AN ADDITIONAL 2 TO 3 MINUTES. REPEAT THIS PROCESS UNTIL ALL OF THE HO CAKES ARE COOKED. SERVE THESE DELICIOUS CAKES WITH YOUR FAVORITE VEGETABLES AND ENJOY A TASTE OF THE SOUTH!

24

FOCACCIA BREAD

 Prep Time
16 Hours

 Cooking Time
25 to 30 Minutes

INGREDIENTS

4 cups bread flour

1 tablespoon kosher salt

1/4 oz instant dry yeast

2 cups warm water

1/2 cup olive oil

TOPPINGS

2 rosemary sprigs

2 cloves garlic thinly sliced

1 teaspoon sea salt

DIRECTIONS 6

IN A LARGE BOWL, MIX TOGETHER FLOUR, SALT, YEAST, AND WATER. USING A RUBBER SPATULA, STIR THE INGREDIENTS UNTIL ALL THE LIQUID IS ABSORBED. KNEAD THE DOUGH FOR ABOUT TWO MINUTES, THEN SHAPE IT INTO A BALL AND PLACE IT IN A SEPARATE BOWL. DRIZZLE ONE TABLESPOON OF OLIVE OIL OVER THE DOUGH TO ENSURE IT IS FULLY COATED. COVER THE BOWL WITH PLASTIC WRAP AND REFRIGERATE FOR 12 HOURS OR OVERNIGHT.

AFTER 12 HOURS, REMOVE THE DOUGH FROM THE REFRIGERATOR AND PLACE IT ON A GREASED BAKING SHEET COATED WITH OLIVE OIL. GENTLY DEFLATE THE DOUGH AND LET IT REST IN THE PAN FOR ANOTHER FOUR HOURS. AFTER THIS TIME, THE DOUGH SHOULD HAVE RISEN AGAIN.

NOW, IT'S TIME TO CREATE DIMPLES IN THE DOUGH. GREASE YOUR HANDS WITH A SMALL AMOUNT OF OLIVE OIL, THEN POUR THE REMAINING OIL OVER THE DOUGH. USE YOUR FINGERS TO CREATE DIMPLES ACROSS THE SURFACE. TOP THE DOUGH WITH VERY THIN SLICES OF GARLIC, SOME PIECES OF ROSEMARY, AND SPRINKLE SEA SALT ON TOP.

BAKE THE DOUGH IN A PREHEATED OVEN AT 375 DEGREES FAHRENHEIT FOR 25 TO 30 MINUTES, OR UNTIL IT IS GOLDEN BROWN. ONCE IT'S OUT OF THE OVEN, SERVE WARM WITH SOME FRESH BUTTER. ENJOY!

FLUFFY BUTTER BISCUITS

 Prep Time 15 Minutes

 Cooking Time 20 TO 25 Minutes

Temp: 375 degrees

INGREDIENTS

**2 cups self-rising flour
(I use White Lilly)
1 tablespoon sugar
1 teaspoon salt
½ cup cold butter
1 cup milk**

DIRECTIONS 8

IN A MEDIUM BOWL, MIX TOGETHER FLOUR, SUGAR, SALT, AND BUTTER WITH YOUR HANDS UNTIL THE MIXTURE HAS THE CONSISTENCY OF CORNMEAL. MAKE A WELL IN THE CENTER OF THE FLOUR MIXTURE AND POUR IN THE MILK. MIX THE DOUGH UNTIL IT COMES TOGETHER, BEING CAREFUL NOT TO OVER-MIX AS IT CAN MAKE THE BISCUITS TOUGH. POUR THE DOUGH ONTO A FLOURED SURFACE AND PRESS IT OUT EVENLY. THEN, FOLD THE DOUGH FROM EACH SIDE, FOLLOWED BY FOLDING THE TOP AND BOTTOM. ONCE THE DOUGH IS FOLDED, PAT IT DOWN INTO A RECTANGLE ABOUT 1/2-INCH THICK. USE A 3-INCH BISCUIT CUTTER TO CUT OUT YOUR BISCUITS. PLACE THE BISCUITS ON A BUTTERED BAKING SHEET OR CAST-IRON PAN. PREHEAT YOUR OVEN TO 375 DEGREES AND BAKE THE BISCUITS FOR 25 MINUTES, OR UNTIL THEY ARE GOLDEN BROWN. SERVE THE BISCUITS HOT WITH SOME STRAWBERRY JAM FOR A DELICIOUS TREAT! ENJOY THE FLAKY GOODNESS OF HOMEMADE BISCUITS WHILE THEY ARE STILL WARM.

Garlic & Cheddar Biscuits

 Prep Time 10 minutes

 Cooking Time
15 Minutes

Oven Temp: 375 degrees

8 to 10

INGREDIENTS

2 cups self-rising flour

1 tablespoon sugar

¼ teaspoon salt

1 teaspoon garlic powder

1 teaspoon 24 herbs and

spices

(I use Bragg)

1/3 cup unsalted butter

1 cup milk or butter milk

1/2 cup sharp cheddar

1/2 cup white sharp

cheddar

1/2 cup Vermont cheddar

Butter Topping

½ stick butter

1 teaspoon garlic powder

1 tablespoon parsley

DIRECTIONS

IN A LARGE BOWL, COMBINE FLOUR, SUGAR, SALT, GARLIC POWDER, AND BRAGG 24 SPICES THOROUGHLY. GRATE BUTTER INTO THE MIXTURE AND BLEND UNTIL IT RESEMBLES CORNMEAL, THEN INCORPORATE THE CHEESE. POUR IN THE MILK AND MIX UNTIL WELL COMBINED. USING A SCOOP, PLACE THE BISCUITS ON A GREASED BAKING SHEET, THEN BAKE AT 375 DEGREES FOR APPROXIMATELY 15 MINUTES UNTIL THEY TURN GOLDEN BROWN. WHILE THE BISCUITS ARE BAKING, PREPARE THE GARLIC BUTTER TOPPING BY MIXING BUTTER, GARLIC, AND PARSLEY IN A BOWL. AFTER THE BISCUITS ARE BAKED, GENEROUSLY BRUSH THEM WITH THE BUTTER MIXTURE. FINALLY, SAVOR THESE DELIGHTFUL BISCUITS.

HONEYBUTTER BISCUITS

 Prep Time 10 Minutes

 Cooking Time 20 TO 25 Minutes

INGREDIENTS

2 cups of all purpose flour

1 tablespoon baking powder

1 tablespoon sugar

1 teaspoon salt

1/4 cup of shortening

1/4 cup butter

2/3 to 3/4 cup milk

Honey Butter Glaze

1/2 cup butter (melted)

1/4 cup honey

DIRECTIONS 🍴 6

LET'S MAKE SOME DELICIOUS HOMEMADE BISCUITS! TO START, GATHER THE NECESSARY INGREDIENTS: FLOUR, BAKING POWDER, SUGAR, SALT, SHORTENING, BUTTER, AND MILK. IN A LARGE BOWL, MIX THE FLOUR, BAKING POWDER, SUGAR, AND SALT TOGETHER. ADD IN THE SHORTENING AND BUTTER, AND MIX UNTIL THE MIXTURE HAS THE CONSISTENCY OF CORN MEAL. THEN, CREATE A WELL IN THE MIDDLE AND POUR IN THE MILK. MIX UNTIL THE DOUGH COMES TOGETHER, BEING CAREFUL NOT TO OVER MIX. SCOOP THE DOUGH ONTO A GREASED BAKING SHEET AND BAKE AT 375 DEGREES FOR 20 TO 25 MINUTES. WHILE THE BISCUITS ARE BAKING, MAKE THE HONEY BUTTER GLAZE BY MIXING MELTED BUTTER AND HONEY IN A SMALL BOWL. ONCE THE BISCUITS ARE DONE, SPREAD THE HONEY BUTTER GLAZE ON TOP AND ENJOY THEM WHILE THEY'RE HOT!

★★★★☆

SOUTHERN CORN BREAD

 Prep Time 10 Minutes

 Cooking Time 25 Minutes

INGREDIENTS

2 cups self rising corn meal

1/3 cup self-rising flour

1/3 cup sugar

2 eggs

1 ½ cup buttermilk

(plus more if needed)

½ cup water

2 tablespoons canola oil

1/3 cup butter

2 tablespoons

DIRECTIONS 6

OR A DELICIOUS AND EASY HOMEMADE CORNBREAD, FOLLOW THESE SIMPLE STEPS. IN A LARGE BOWL, COMBINE CORN MEAL, SELF-RISING FLOUR, SUGAR, EGGS, BUTTERMILK, AND WATER. MIX WELL UNTIL ALL THE INGREDIENTS ARE FULLY INCORPORATED. IN A SEPARATE CAST IRON PAN, MELT 2 TABLESPOONS OF CANOLA OIL AND 1/3 CUP OF BUTTER. ONCE MELTED, POUR THE MIXTURE INTO THE CORNBREAD BATTER AND MIX WELL. THEN, POUR THE BATTER BACK INTO THE CAST IRON PAN AND PLACE IT IN A PREHEATED 375 DEGREE OVEN FOR 20 TO 25 MINUTES, OR UNTIL GOLDEN BROWN. ONCE DONE, REMOVE FROM THE OVEN AND SPREAD THE REMAINING 2 TABLESPOONS OF BUTTER OVER THE TOP OF THE CORNBREAD. SERVE HOT AND ENJOY THIS DELICIOUS HOMEMADE TREAT.

YEAST ROLLS

 Prep Time 15 Minutes

 Cooking Time 20 TO 25 Minutes

 Poof Time 1 Hour 45 Minutes

Temp: 375 degrees

INGREDIENTS

1 1/4 cup lukewarm

whole milk

4 teaspoons active dry yeast

4 cups bread flour

1/2 cup sugar

1 teaspoon salt

2 large eggs (beaten)

4 tablespoons butter

DIRECTIONS 8

IN A SMALL BOWL, COMBINE THE LUKEWARM 2% MILK AND ACTIVE DRY YEAST, ALLOWING THE MIXTURE TO REST FOR APPROXIMATELY 5 MINUTES UNTIL IT BECOMES FROTHY. IN A LARGE MIXING BOWL, COMBINE THE BREAD FLOUR, SUGAR, AND SALT, MAKING A WELL IN THE CENTER OF THE DRY INGREDIENTS. INTO THE WELL, ADD THE BEATEN EGGS AND THE YEAST MIXTURE. STIR UNTIL A DOUGH BEGINS TO FORM. INTEGRATE THE BUTTER INTO THE DOUGH AND KNEAD ON A FLOURED SURFACE FOR APPROXIMATELY 8-10 MINUTES, OR UNTIL THE DOUGH BECOMES SMOOTH AND ELASTIC. PLACE THE DOUGH IN A GREASED BOWL, COVER IT WITH A CLEAN KITCHEN TOWEL, AND ALLOW IT TO RISE IN A WARM LOCATION FOR APPROXIMATELY 1-2 HOURS, OR UNTIL IT HAS DOUBLED IN SIZE. ONCE THE DOUGH HAS RISEN, PUNCH IT DOWN TO RELEASE THE AIR. DIVIDE THE DOUGH INTO EQUAL PORTIONS AND SHAPE THEM INTO INDIVIDUAL ROLLS OR PLACE THEM INTO A BREAD LOAF PAN. COVER THE SHAPED DOUGH AND ALLOW IT TO RISE AGAIN FOR ANOTHER 30-45 MINUTES. PREHEAT YOUR OVEN TO 375°F (190°C). BAKE THE BREAD FOR APPROXIMATELY 25-30 MINUTES, OR UNTIL IT IS GOLDEN BROWN AND SOUNDS HOLLOW WHEN TAPPED ON THE BOTTOM. LET THE BREAD COOL SLIGHTLY BEFORE SLICING AND SERVING. ENJOY YOUR FRESHLY BAKED ROLLS!

LOVE

Love is a profound and multifaceted emotion that encompasses a range of feelings, from deep affection and attachment to passion and commitment. It can manifest in various forms, such as the unconditional love between family members, the supportive and caring love between friends, or the romantic love that binds partners together. Love involves a sense of protectiveness, warmth, and trust, creating a bond that often transcends time and challenges. It is a driving force that inspires acts of kindness, sacrifice, and compassion, making it one of the most powerful and cherished experiences.

BREAKFAST

BACON & SPINACH FRITTATA

 Prep Time 1O Minutes

 Cooking Time 25 Minutes

INGREDIENTS

8 large Eggs

¼ cup water

8 strips of bacon

(cut into pieces)

1 medium onion (Diced)

3 cups spinach

1 cup tomatoes

1 cup shredded sharp

cheddar cheese.

salt and pepper to taste

DIRECTIONS 6

CUT THE BACON AND ONION INTO PIECES. CRACK THE EGGS INTO A BOWL, THEN ADD WATER, SALT, AND PEPPER, SETTING IT ASIDE. COOK THE BACON IN A PAN UNTIL IT BECOMES CRISPY, THEN REMOVE AND SET IT ASIDE. DRAIN MOST OF THE BACON GREASE FROM THE PAN, LEAVING ABOUT 1 TABLESPOON. NEXT, SAUTÉ THE ONIONS UNTIL THEY TURN TRANSLUCENT, FOLLOWED BY ADDING THE SPINACH AND LETTING IT COOK DOWN. POUR THE EGG MIXTURE OVER THE COOKED VEGETABLES, ENSURING AN EVEN DISTRIBUTION IN THE PAN. ADD THE BACON, TOMATOES, AND SHARP CHEDDAR CHEESE, MIXING EVERYTHING THOROUGHLY. TRANSFER THE PAN TO THE OVEN AT 350 DEGREES FOR 25 TO 30 MINUTES. ONCE DONE, REMOVE FROM THE OVEN AND LET IT REST FOR 5 MINUTES BEFORE SERVING. ENJOY YOUR MEAL!

BLUEBERRY BISCUITS

 Prep Time 1O Minutes

 Cooking Time 15 to 20 Minutes

INGREDIENTS

2 cups self-rising flour

1 tablespoon sugar

1/2 cup butter

1 cup milk

1 cup blueberries

The Glaze

2 cups of

confection sugar

1 teaspoon of butter

1/2 teaspoon of vanilla

3 to 4 tablespoons

of milk

DIRECTIONS 6

OLLOW THESE EASY STEPS TO MAKE DELICIOUS BLUEBERRY BISCUITS. IN A LARGE BOWL, COMBINE FLOUR AND SUGAR, THEN MIX WELL. ADD IN THE BUTTER AND MIX WITH YOUR HANDS UNTIL THE MIXTURE IS THE CONSISTENCY OF CORNMEAL. GRADUALLY ADD IN THE MILK AND MIX UNTIL FULLY INCORPORATED, BEING CAREFUL NOT TO OVER MIX. GENTLY FOLD IN THE BLUEBERRIES WITH A SPATULA. USING A MEDIUM SCOOP, PLACE THE BISCUITS ONTO A GREASED BAKING SHEET AND BAKE IN THE OVEN FOR 20 TO 25 MINUTES, OR UNTIL THEY ARE GOLDEN BROWN. WHILE THE BISCUITS ARE BAKING, MAKE THE GLAZE BY COMBINING CONFECTIONERS' SUGAR, BUTTER, VANILLA, AND MILK IN A SMALL BOWL. MIX UNTIL WELL INCORPORATED. ONCE THE BISCUITS ARE DONE, SPREAD THE GLAZE ALL OVER THEM AND ENJOY YOUR DELICIOUS, HOMEMADE BLUEBERRY BISCUITS.

 9x13 inch

BLUEBERRY PANCAKES

 Prep Time 1O Minutes

 Cooking Time 15 Minutes

INGREDIENTS

2 cups all purpose flour

1/8 cup sugar

1 tablespoon baking powder

½ teaspoon baking soda

½ teaspoon salt

1 1/4 cup milk

1 large egg

1 tablespoon vanilla

1 tablespoon butter

1 cup fresh blueberries

DIRECTIONS 4

TO PREPARE THESE DELIGHTFUL BLUEBERRY PANCAKES, BEGIN BY COMBINING FLOUR, SUGAR, BAKING POWDER, SALT, MILK, AND EGGS IN A MEDIUM BOWL, MIXING THOROUGHLY. IN A SEPARATE BOWL, WHISK TOGETHER THE EGGS, BUTTER, MILK, AND VANILLA. POUR THE WET MIXTURE INTO THE DRY INGREDIENTS AND BLEND WELL.

NEXT, HEAT A MEDIUM SKILLET OVER MEDIUM HEAT. TO CHECK IF IT'S READY, SPRINKLE A FEW DROPS OF WATER ONTO THE SURFACE; IF THEY DANCE AROUND, YOU'RE GOOD TO GO. ADD A LITTLE MELTED BUTTER TO THE SKILLET AND USE A ¼ CUP MEASURING CUP TO SCOOP THE BATTER ONTO THE SKILLET, FORMING APPROXIMATELY 4-INCH CIRCLES.

SPRINKLE SOME BLUEBERRY EVENLY OVER THE PANCAKES. COOK FOR 1 TO 2 MINUTES, OR UNTIL BUBBLES BEGIN TO FORM AND THE EDGES TURN BROWN, THEN FLIP TO COOK THE OTHER SIDE FOR AN ADDITIONAL 1 TO 2 MINUTES UNTIL GOLDEN BROWN. REMOVE FROM THE SKILLET, TOP WITH SYRUP, AND ENJOY!

FRENCH TOAST

 Prep Time 10 Minutes

 Cooking Time 5 Minutes

DIRECTIONS 4

TO PREPARE THIS DELICIOUS FRENCH TOAST, START BY COMBINING THE MILK, EGG, CINNAMON, AND SUGAR IN A MEDIUM BOWL, MIXING THOROUGHLY. NEXT, HEAT A MEDIUM SKILLET OVER MEDIUM HEAT AND ADD THE BUTTER. TAKE EACH SLICE OF BREAD AND IMMERSE IT IN THE MILK MIXTURE, ENSURING BOTH SIDES ARE WELL-COATED. PLACE THE COATED BREAD IN THE HOT SKILLET AND COOK FOR ABOUT 1 TO 2 MINUTES UNTIL BROWNED, THEN FLIP IT OVER. COOK FOR AN ADDITIONAL 1 TO 2 MINUTES UNTIL GOLDEN BROWN, THEN REMOVE FROM THE SKILLET. FINISH BY SPRINKLING WITH POWDERED SUGAR AND DRIZZLING WITH SYRUP. ENJOY YOUR DELIGHTFUL CREATION!

INGREDIENTS

4 pieces thick cut brioche bread

1 cup milk

1 egg

1 tablespoons cinnamon

1 tablespoon sugar

2 tablespoons butter

¼ cup powdered sugar.

1 cup heated syrup

★★★★☆

SAUSAGE GRAVY

 Prep Time 5 Minutes

 Cooking Time
15 Minutes

INGREDIENTS

1lb. ground pork sausage

2 tablespoons butter

1/4 cup all purpose flour

2 cups milk

½ cup water

½ teaspoon salt

1 teaspoon pepper

DIRECTIONS 4

IN A LARGE SKILLET, ADD THE GROUND PORK AND COOK IT UNTIL FULLY BROWNED. ONCE COOKED, INCORPORATE THE FLOUR AND SAUTÉ FOR ABOUT 1 TO 2 MINUTES TO ELIMINATE THE RAW FLOUR TASTE. NEXT, STIR IN THE MILK AND WATER, CONTINUING TO MIX UNTIL THE MIXTURE THICKENS INTO A GRAVY. THEN, SEASON WITH SALT AND PEPPER, ALLOWING IT TO COOK FOR AN ADDITIONAL ONE TO TWO MINUTES. SERVE IT HOT OVER A FRESHLY BAKED BISCUIT AND ENJOY!

♥

TEACHING IS A WORK OF HEART

STRAWBERRY BISCUITS

 Prep Time 1O Minutes

 Cooking Time 15 TO 20 Minutes

INGREDIENTS

2 cup self rising flour

1 tablespoon sugar

1/2 cup butter

1 cup milk

1 cup chopped strawberries

The Glaze

1 cup confectioners sugar

1 teaspoon melted butter

1/2 teaspoon vanilla

2 tablespoon milk or more

(make it smooth)

DIRECTIONS 6

THESE DELICIOUS STRAWBERRY BISCUITS ARE MADE EXACTLY THE SAME WAY AS THE BLUEBERRY BISCUITS. . IN A LARGE BOWL, COMBINE FLOUR AND SUGAR, THEN MIX WELL. ADD IN THE BUTTER AND MIX WITH YOUR HANDS UNTIL THE MIXTURE IS THE CONSISTENCY OF CORNMEAL. GRADUALLY ADD IN THE MILK AND MIX UNTIL FULLY INCORPORATED, BEING CAREFUL NOT TO OVER MIX. GENTLY FOLD IN THE STRAWBERRIES WITH A SPATULA. USING A MEDIUM SCOOP, PLACE THE BISCUITS ONTO A GREASED BAKING SHEET AND BAKE IN THE OVEN FOR 20 TO 25 MINUTES, OR UNTIL THEY ARE GOLDEN BROWN. WHILE THE BISCUITS ARE BAKING, MAKE THE GLAZE BY COMBINING CONFECTIONERS' SUGAR, BUTTER, VANILLA, AND MILK IN A SMALL BOWL. MIX UNTIL WELL INCORPORATED. ONCE THE BISCUITS ARE DONE, SPREAD THE GLAZE ALL OVER THEM AND ENJOY YOUR DELICIOUS STRAWBERRY BISCUITS.

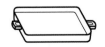 9x13 inch

STRAWBERRY PANCAKES

 Prep Time 15 Minutes

 Cooking Time 15 Minutes

INGREDIENTS

2 cups all purpose flour

1/8 cup sugar

1 tablespoon baking powder

½ teaspoon baking soda

½ teaspoon salt

1 1/4 cup milk

1 large egg

1 tablespoon vanilla

1 tablespoon butter

1 cup fresh strawberries

DIRECTIONS 4

TO PREPARE THESE DELIGHTFUL STRAWBERRY PANCAKES, BEGIN BY COMBINING FLOUR, SUGAR, BAKING POWDER, SALT, MILK, AND EGGS IN A MEDIUM BOWL, MIXING THOROUGHLY. IN A SEPARATE BOWL, WHISK TOGETHER THE EGGS, BUTTER, MILK, AND VANILLA. POUR THE WET MIXTURE INTO THE DRY INGREDIENTS AND BLEND WELL.

NEXT, HEAT A MEDIUM SKILLET OVER MEDIUM HEAT. TO CHECK IF IT'S READY, SPRINKLE A FEW DROPS OF WATER ONTO THE SURFACE; IF THEY DANCE AROUND, YOU'RE GOOD TO GO. ADD A LITTLE MELTED BUTTER TO THE SKILLET AND USE A ¼ CUP MEASURING CUP TO SCOOP THE BATTER ONTO THE SKILLET, FORMING APPROXIMATELY 4-INCH CIRCLES.

SPRINKLE SOME STRAWBERRIES EVENLY OVER THE PANCAKES. COOK FOR 1 TO 2 MINUTES, OR UNTIL BUBBLES BEGIN TO FORM AND THE EDGES TURN BROWN, THEN FLIP TO COOK THE OTHER SIDE FOR AN ADDITIONAL 1 TO 2 MINUTES UNTIL GOLDEN BROWN. REMOVE FROM THE SKILLET, TOP WITH SYRUP, AND ENJOY!

WHITE PEPPER GRAVY

 Prep Time 1O Minutes

 Cooking Time 15 Minutes

INGREDIENTS

2 to 3 tablespoons of oil
or bacon grease

4 tablespoons all-purpose
flour

2 cup whole milk

1 teaspoon salt

1 teaspoon onion powder

1 tablespoon pepper

DIRECTIONS 6

TO ACHIEVE A SMOOTH AND TASTY GRAVY, IT IS IMPORTANT TO COOK THE FLOUR PROPERLY.IN A LARGE SKILLET, HEAT UP SOME BACON GREASE AND ADD IN THE FLOUR, MAKING SURE TO MIX IT WELL. COOK FOR ABOUT 1 TO 2 MINUTES, BEING CAREFUL NOT TO LET THE FLOUR TURN BROWN. THIS WILL HELP TO GET RID OF THE RAW FLOUR TASTE. THEN, SLOWLY POUR IN THE MILK AND STIR CONTINUOUSLY UNTIL THE GRAVY THICKENS. YOU CAN ADD MORE MILK IF NEEDED TO REACH YOUR DESIRED CONSISTENCY. FINALLY, SEASON WITH SOME SALT, PEPPER, AND ONION POWDER FOR ADDED FLAVOR. SERVE THIS DELICIOUS HOMEMADE GRAVY WITH SOME HOT BISCUITS FOR A COMFORTING AND SATISFYING MEAL.

KELLZ REFLECTION

As a young girl, I lovingly recall the warm, bustling kitchen where I spent endless hours cooking alongside my mom and grandmother. The delightful scents of freshly baked bread and simmering soups filled the air, creating a cozy ambiance. I treasured the times my grandmother patiently taught me how to knead dough, while my mom shared cherished family recipes passed down through generations. The kitchen was a haven of laughter, love, and learning, where three generations connected through the simple pleasure of cooking together. These memories have become a beloved part of my childhood, reminding me of our strong family bonds and the joy found in preparing meals.

SOUPS & SALADS

BEEF & VEGETABLE STEW

 Prep Time 20 Minutes

Cooking Time
2 Hours 30 Minutes

DIRECTIONS 6

INGREDIENTS

2 lbs. stew beef

1 whole onion chopped

4 stalks celery chopped

3 carrots chopped

1 green bell pepper

1 red bell pepper

1 orange bell pepper

1 yellow bell pepper

1.5lb. honey gold potatoes

3 cloves garlic chopped

2 cups sweet peas

2 tablespoons olive oil

1 tablespoon creole seasoning

1 tablespoon garlic powder

1 tablespoon onion powder

1 tablespoon caramelized onion butter (I use Kinder's)

Salt and pepper to taste

1 tablespoon tomato paste

1 cup crushed tomatoes

6 cups beef broth or

1 tablespoon butter the bullion

1 tablespoon thyme

1 tablespoon rosemary

2 bay leaves

Cornstarch Slurry

1 tablespoon cornstarch

2 tablespoons water

TO CREATE THIS DELICIOUS BEEF AND VEGETABLE STEW, START BY HEATING OLIVE OIL IN A LARGE POT OVER MEDIUM HEAT. ONCE THE OIL IS HOT, ADD THE BEEF AND SEASON IT WITH CREOLE SEASONING, GARLIC POWDER, ONION POWDER, AND CARAMELIZED ONION BUTTER. SEAR THE BEEF UNTIL IT'S BROWNED, THEN TAKE IT OUT OF THE POT. IN THE SAME POT, ADD ONIONS, CARROTS, CELERY, AND PEPPERS, SEASONING THEM WITH SALT AND PEPPER. SAUTÉ THE VEGETABLES UNTIL THEY BECOME TENDER, THEN STIR IN THE GARLIC AND TOMATO PASTE, COOKING FOR ABOUT A MINUTE UNTIL AROMATIC. RETURN THE BEEF TO THE POT AND MIX IN CRUSHED TOMATOES, BEEF BROTH, BEEF BETTER THAN BOUILLON, THYME, ROSEMARY, AND BAY LEAVES. COVER THE POT AND LET IT SIMMER FOR 1 ½ HOURS, OR UNTIL THE BEEF IS TENDER. NEXT, ADD PEAS AND POTATOES, COVER AGAIN, AND REDUCE THE HEAT TO A LOW SIMMER, COOKING FOR AN ADDITIONAL 30 TO 45 MINUTES UNTIL THE POTATOES ARE SOFT. REMOVE THE BAY LEAVES AND STIR IN THE CORNSTARCH SLURRY (MADE FROM CORNSTARCH AND WATER), COOKING FOR ANOTHER 10 MINUTES UNTIL THE CORNSTARCH FLAVOR HAS BLENDED IN. SERVE THE STEW ALONGSIDE WHITE RICE AND CORNBREAD FOR A DELIGHTFUL MEAL. ENJOY!

★★★★☆

Broccli & Cheddar Soup

Prep Time 15 minutes

Cooking Time
25 Minutes

4

INGREDIENTS

1/4 cup butter

1 cup chopped onions

1 stalks chopped celery

1 cup shredded carrots

1 teaspoon garlic paste

¼ cup all-purpose flour

2 cups chicken broth

2 cups half and half

3 cups chopped broccoli

1 chicken bouillon packet

1 teaspoon garlic powder

1 teaspoon onion powder

1 teaspoon paprika

Salt and pepper to taste

1 cup shredded Monterey

Jack Cheese

1 cup cheddar cheese

DIRECTIONS

TO MAKE BROCCOLI AND CHEESE SOUP, START BY SETTING YOUR POT TO MEDIUM HEAT AND ADDING IN THE BUTTER, ONIONS, CELERY, AND CARROTS COOK UNTIL CARROTS ARE ALMOST TENDER AND THE ONIONS ARE TRANSLUCENT. THEN, ADD IN THE GARLIC PASTE AND COOK FOR ABOUT ONE MINUTE, JUST UNTIL THE GARLIC IS FRAGRANT. NEXT, ADD IN THE FLOUR AND LET IT COOK FOR 2 TO 3 MINUTES TO REMOVE THE FLOUR TASTE. POUR IN THE CHICKEN BROTH AND HALF AND HALF AND STIR UNTIL IT THICKENS. NOW ADD IN THE BROCCOLI, CHICKEN BOUILLON PACKET, GARLIC POWDER, ONION POWDER, PAPRIKA, SALT, AND PEPPER. GIVE IT A QUICK STIR AND THEN ADD IN THE CHEESE. STIR UNTIL THE CHEESE IS FULLY MELTED. COVER THE POT AND LET IT SIMMER FOR 20 MINUTES, STIRRING OCCASIONALLY TO AVOID STICKING. AND VOILA, YOUR DELICIOUS BROCCOLI AND CHEESE SOUP IS READY TO BE ENJOYED!

BUFFALO CHICKEN SALAD

 Prep Time 15 Minutes

 Cooking Time 12 TO 15 Minutes

INGREDIENTS

2 chicken breasts (cut into chunks)

1 tablespoon creole seasoning

1 tablespoon roasted garlic powder

1 tablespoon onion powder

1 tablespoon paprika

2 ½ cups flour

1 cup water

Buffalo Sauce

1 cup hot sauce

½ cup butter

1 teaspoon roasted garlic powder

1 teaspoon onion powder

1 teaspoon paprika

1 teaspoon chili powder

Build The Salad

Lettuce

Tomato

Cucumber

Onions

Blue cheese Crumbles

Croutons

Blue Cheese Dressing

DIRECTIONS 3

BEGIN BY PREPARING THE SEASONING MIX IN A SMALL BOWL, COMBINING CREOLE SEASONING, ROASTED GARLIC POWDER, ONION POWDER, AND PAPRIKA.IN A SEPARATE LARGE BOWL, COAT THE CHICKEN CHUNKS WITH HALF OF THE SEASONING MIX, 1/2 CUP FLOUR, AND WATER. IN ANOTHER LARGE BOWL, MIX 2 CUPS OF FLOUR WITH THE REMAINING SEASONING MIX. PREHEAT THE OIL TO 365 DEGREES AND FRY THE CHICKEN FOR 10 TO 12 MINUTES UNTIL GOLDEN BROWN. WHILE THE CHICKEN IS DRAINING ON A RACK, MAKE THE DELICIOUS SAUCE BY MELTING BUTTER IN A PYREX CUP AND ADDING HOT SAUCE, ONION POWDER, GARLIC POWDER, PAPRIKA, AND CHILI POWDER. POUR THE SAUCE OVER THE CHICKEN AND MIX WELL. ASSEMBLE THE SALAD BY ADDING LETTUCE, TOMATOES, CUCUMBERS, ONIONS, BLUE CHEESE CRUMBLES, AND CROUTONS ON A PLATE. TOP IT OFF WITH THE BUFFALO CHICKEN AND DRIZZLE HOMEMADE BLUE CHEESE DRESSING FOR A TRULY SATISFYING MEAL.

CHICKEN & CORN CHOWDER

 Prep Time 15 Minutes

 Cooking Time 30 Minutes

INGREDIENTS

1/2 stick butter

1 onion chopped

1 red pepper chopped

1 yellow pepper chopped

3 garlic chopped

3 large potatoes

chopped

1 whole rotisserie

chicken

(shredded)

2 cups fresh corn

1 teaspoon garlic

powder

1 teaspoon onion

powder

1 teaspoon onion powder

1 teaspoon thyme

1 teaspoon salt

1 teaspoon pepper

2 bay leaves

1 cup heavy cream

The Slurry

1 tablespoon cornstarch

1 tablespoon water

Garnish

Bacon Bits

Green Onions

1 tablespoon parsley

DIRECTIONS 4

TO PREPARE THIS DELIGHTFUL CHICKEN CORN CHOWDER, START BY HEATING A LARGE POT OVER MEDIUM HEAT. ADD THE BUTTER, ONIONS, RED PEPPERS, YELLOW PEPPERS, GARLIC, POTATOES, CHICKEN, CORN, AND CHICKEN STOCK, MIXING EVERYTHING TOGETHER THOROUGHLY. ALLOW IT TO COOK UNTIL THE POTATOES ARE TENDER, WHICH SHOULD TAKE ABOUT 8 MINUTES. NEXT, STIR IN THE GARLIC POWDER, ONION POWDER, THYME, SALT, PEPPER, AND BAY LEAVES. INCORPORATE THE HEAVY CREAM AND THE SLURRY; ONCE IT THICKENS, REDUCE THE HEAT AND LET IT SIMMER FOR 20 MINUTES. FINALLY, SERVE IT IN A BOWL, TOPPING IT WITH BACON BITS, GREEN ONIONS, AND PARSLEY, AND SAVOR EVERY BITE!

CHICKEN & DUMPLINGS

 Prep Time 20 minutes

 Cooking Time
2 hours

🍴 6

INGREDIENTS

1 whole chicken cut up

3 carrots cut into pieces

2 tablespoons creole seasoning

3 stalks of celery cut into pieces

1 whole sweet onion chopped

into pieces

2 tablespoons olive oil

3 cloves garlic chopped

3 cups water

¼ cup chicken better than bouillon

2 sprigs fresh thyme

1 sprig fresh rosemary

2 bay leaves

1 chicken bouillon packet

½ stick butter

1 tablespoon black pepper

2 tablespoons parsley

1/3 cup heavy cream

The Dumplings

1 ½ cup all-purpose flour

1 tablespoon baking powder

1 teaspoon sugar

1/ 2 teaspoon salt

1 teaspoon garlic powder

1 tablespoon dried parsley

2 tablespoons melted butter

½ to ¾ cup milk

DIRECTIONS

TO PREPARE CHICKEN AND DUMPLINGS, COMMENCE BY SEASONING THE CHICKEN ON ALL SIDES WITH CREOLE SEASONING. NEXT, HEAT OLIVE OIL IN A DUTCH OVEN AND SEAR THE CHICKEN, SKIN SIDE DOWN, UNTIL BROWNED ON ALL SIDES. REMOVE THE CHICKEN, THEN SAUTÉ ONIONS, CELERY, AND CARROTS UNTIL TENDER, FOLLOWED BY GARLIC FOR ONE MINUTE. RETURN THE CHICKEN TO THE POT, ADDING WATER, BETTER THAN BOUILLON PACKET, THYME, AND BAY LEAVES. BRING TO A BOIL, THEN REDUCE HEAT AND SIMMER FOR TWO HOURS OR UNTIL THE CHICKEN REACHES 165°F. MEANWHILE, PREPARE DUMPLINGS BY COMBINING FLOUR, BAKING POWDER, SUGAR, SALT, GARLIC POWDER, PARSLEY, BUTTER, AND MILK IN A BOWL. ONCE THE CHICKEN IS TENDER, SHRED AND RETURN IT TO THE POT, DISCARDING BONES AND SKIN. REMOVE BAY LEAVES AND THYME STEMS, THEN ADD CHICKEN BOUILLON PACKET, BUTTER, PEPPER, AND PARSLEY. SCOOP DUMPLINGS INTO THE POT, ENSURING SEPARATION,ADD IN THE HEAVY CREAM AND SIMMER FOR 15 MINUTES OR UNTIL DOUBLED IN SIZE AND FLUFFY. SERVE DUMPLINGS IN A BOWL AND ENJOY!

HAMBURGER SOUP

 Prep Time 15 Minutes

 Cooking Time 40 Minutes

INGREDIENTS

3 lbs. ground beef
1 tablespoon olive oil
1 medium onion diced 24 oz
mixed veggies
3 - 14.5 oz cans diced
tomatoes
2 cups beef broth
1 tablespoon onion powder
1 tablespoon garlic powder
1 tablespoon creole
seasoning
1 tablespoon thyme
1 tablespoon rosemary
salt and pepper to taste
2 bay leaves

DIRECTIONS 6

TO PREPARE HAMBURGER SOUP, START BY COOKING GROUND BEEF IN A LARGE POT UNTIL IT'S BROWNED. ONCE DONE, REMOVE THE BEEF TO DRAIN ANY EXCESS OIL. NEXT, ADD OLIVE OIL AND ONIONS TO THE POT, COOKING FOR ABOUT THREE MINUTES TO ENHANCE THE FLAVOR OF THE ONIONS. AFTER ADDING BEEF BROTH, SEASON THE MIXTURE WITH ONION POWDER, GARLIC POWDER, CREOLE SEASONING, THYME, ROSEMARY, SALT, AND PEPPER. THEN, INCORPORATE MIXED VEGETABLES, TOMATOES, AND BAY LEAVES. COVER THE POT AND LET IT SIMMER ON MEDIUM-LOW HEAT FOR 40 MINUTES. BEFORE SERVING, BE SURE TO REMOVE THE BAY LEAVES AND SAVOR YOUR DELICIOUS MEAL!

ITALIAN PASTA SALAD

 Prep Time
25 Minutes

 Cooking Time
7 Minutes

INGREDIENTS

1 pound of tricolored
rotini pasta
1 cup chopped red
onion
1 cup chopped bell
peppers
1 cup chopped roasted
red peppers
1 cup black olives
1 cup salad olives

8 oz pack of
cheddar cheese
(cubes)
8 oz pack pepper
jack cheese (cubes)
1 zesty Italian
seasoning packet
1/4 c. red wine
vinegar
1/4 c. EVOO- extra
virgin olive oil
1 16oz bottle of
Olive Garden salad
dressing

DIRECTIONS 8

BEGIN BY BRINGING A POT OF WATER TO A BOIL
OVER HIGH HEAT. ONCE BOILING, ADD THE PASTA
AND COOK UNTIL AL DENTE, WHICH TAKES ABOUT
7 MINUTES. AFTER COOKING, REMOVE THE PASTA,
DRAIN IT, AND TRANSFER IT TO A LARGE MIXING
BOWL. ALLOW IT TO COOL FOR APPROXIMATELY 10
MINUTES. THEN, INCORPORATE THE ONIONS, BELL
PEPPERS, ROASTED RED PEPPERS, BLACK OLIVES,
SALAD OLIVES, CHEDDAR CHEESE, PEPPER JACK
CHEESE, THE ITALIAN SEASONING PACKET, RED
WINE VINEGAR, EXTRA VIRGIN OLIVE OIL, AND THE
ENTIRE BOTTLE OF OLIVE GARDEN SALAD
DRESSING. MIX EVERYTHING THOROUGHLY.
COVER THE BOWL AND LET THE PASTA SALAD
ABSORB ALL THE FLAVORS. YOU CAN SERVE IT
WARM OR REFRIGERATE FOR AN HOUR TO ENJOY
IT COLD. NOW, SAVOR YOUR DELICIOUS CREATION!

TORTILLA SOUP

 Prep Time
20 Minutes

 Cooking Time
50 Minutes

INGREDIENTS

2 tablespoons olive oil

1 whole rotisserie
chicken

1 cup onions

2 cloves garlic chopped

1 cup black beans
(drained and washed)

1 14.5 oz can fire roasted
diced tomatoes

32oz chicken stock

1 teaspoon garlic
powder

1 teaspoon onion
powder

1 teaspoon onion powder
1 teaspoon cumin
1 teaspoon chili powder
1 teaspoon paprika
1 teaspoon salt
1 teaspoon pepper
2 bay leaves
1/4 cup fresh lime juice
4 flour or corn tortillas
cut into strips
Toppings
1 cup Mexican cheese
blend
1 avocado
1 cup cilantro
fresh squeezed lemon
juice.

DIRECTIONS 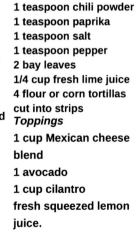 4

IN A LARGE POT SET OVER MEDIUM HEAT, POUR IN SOME OLIVE OIL AND THEN ADD THE ONIONS. SAUTÉ THE ONIONS UNTIL THEY BECOME TRANSLUCENT, THEN INCORPORATE THE GARLIC. COOK THE ONIONS AND GARLIC TOGETHER UNTIL THE GARLIC IS FRAGRANT, ABOUT ONE MINUTE. NEXT, ADD THE BLACK BEANS AND ROASTED TOMATOES, MIXING EVERYTHING WELL BEFORE INTRODUCING THE SEASONINGS. STIR IN GARLIC POWDER, ONION POWDER, CHILI POWDER, PAPRIKA, CUMIN, SALT, AND PEPPER.

THEN, POUR IN THE CHICKEN STOCK AND ADD THE CHICKEN, ALLOWING THE MIXTURE TO COME TO A BOIL. ONCE BOILING, TOSS IN THE BAY LEAVES AND COVER THE POT WITH A LID. REDUCE THE HEAT AND LET IT SIMMER FOR ABOUT 30 MINUTES. AFTER 30 MINUTES, ADD THE CORNSTARCH SLURRY (A MIXTURE OF CORNSTARCH AND WATER) AND STIR CONTINUOUSLY UNTIL THE SOUP THICKENS. FOR A TOUCH OF FRESHNESS, ADD LIME JUICE AND LOWER THE HEAT TO A GENTLE SIMMER.

WHILE THE SOUP SIMMERS, PREPARE THE CHIPS. IN A LARGE SKILLET OVER MEDIUM HEAT, ADD A SHALLOW LAYER OF OIL. ONCE HEATED, ADD THE CHIPS, KEEPING A CLOSE EYE ON THEM AS THEY CAN BROWN QUICKLY. ONCE THEY ARE ALL BROWNED, TRANSFER THEM TO A COOLING RACK AND SALT THEM IMMEDIATELY.

TO SERVE, LADLE THE SOUP INTO A BOWL, ADD SOME CHIPS, AND TOP WITH CHEESE, AVOCADOS, CILANTRO, AND A SQUEEZE OF LIME JUICE. ENJOY YOUR DELICIOUS CREATION!

57

TRIDITIONAL CHICKEN SALAD

 Prep Time 15 Minutes

INGREDIENTS

 2

1 whole rotisserie chicken
3 stalks celery (chopped)
1/2 onion chopped (chopped)
1/2 cup sweet relish
1/2 to 3/4 cups mayonnaise
1 teaspoon garlic pepper seasoning

1 teaspoon onion powder
salt and pepper to taste
ADD ONS
Roma tomatoes
Green leaf lettuce
English Cucumber
Artisan collection crackers
(harvest wheat classic butter crisp rosemary & olive oil)

DIRECTIONS

TO PREPARE THIS DELICIOUS CHICKEN SALAD, BEGIN BY SHREDDING THE CHICKEN INTO A LARGE BOWL. NEXT, INCORPORATE THE CHOPPED CELERY, ONIONS, SWEET RELISH, MAYONNAISE, GARLIC PEPPER SEASONING, ONION POWDER, AND SALT AND PEPPER. MIX ALL THE INGREDIENTS THOROUGHLY. SERVE THE SALAD OVER A BED OF LETTUCE, GARNISHING IT WITH ROMA TOMATOES AND ENGLISH CUCUMBERS. PAIR IT WITH ARTISAN CRACKERS AND SAVOR THE FLAVORS!

MANIFESTATION

Manifestation is the process of bringing your desires and goals into reality through focused intention, belief, and action. It is based on the idea that our thoughts and emotions have the power to shape our experiences and the world around us. By visualizing what you want to achieve, maintaining a positive mindset, and taking consistent steps towards your goals, you can attract the opportunities and resources needed to make your dreams come true. Manifestation often involves practices such as affirmations, visualization techniques, and gratitude, which help align your energy with your aspirations. Ultimately, it is about harnessing the power of your mind and the universe to create the life you envision.

MAIN COURSES

AIRFRYER RIBS

 Prep Time 15 Minutes

 Cooking Time 1 Hour 25 Minutes

INGREDIENTS

1 slab baby back ribs

1 tablespoon creole seasoning

1 tablespoon paprika

1 tablespoon chili powder

1 tablespoon onion powder

1 tablespoon garlic

1 tablespoon dry-mustard

1/4 cup brown sugar

DIRECTIONS 4

TO PREPARE THESE MOUTHWATERING RIBS, START BY CLEANING THEM AND REMOVING THE MEMBRANE FROM THE BACK. IN A SMALL BOWL, COMBINE THE CREOLE SEASONING, PAPRIKA, CHILI POWDER, ONION POWDER, GARLIC POWDER, DRY MUSTARD, AND SUGAR. GENEROUSLY RUB THIS MIXTURE ALL OVER THE RIBS. PREHEAT YOUR AIR FRYER TO 375 DEGREES FAHRENHEIT. PLACE THE RIBS ON A BAKING RACK AND COOK FOR 30 MINUTES, THEN FLIP THEM OVER. RETURN THE RIBS TO THE AIR FRYER FOR AN ADDITIONAL 30 MINUTES. ONCE THE INTERNAL TEMPERATURE REACHES 170 DEGREES, TAKE THEM OUT OF THE AIR FRYER. SLATHER YOUR FAVORITE BBQ SAUCE OVER THE RIBS AND PLACE THEM BACK IN THE AIR FRYER FOR ANOTHER 25 MINUTES. FINALLY, REMOVE THEM FROM THE AIR FRYER AND ENJOY!

★★★★☆

BEEF & GRAVY

 Prep Time 15
Minutes

 Cooking Time
25 TO 35 Minutes

INGREDIENTS

3lbs ground beef

1 onion chopped

2 tablespoon minced garlic

2 tablespoons minced onion

**2 tablespoons Steak King
Chophouse Blend**

¼ cup Worcestershire sauce

1 egg

1 tablespoon pepper

Salt (optional)

The Gravy

4 tablespoon olive oil

1/4 cup flour

2 cup water

1 teaspoon beef bouillon

Pepper to taste

DIRECTIONS 8

TO PREPARE BEEF AND GRAVY, START WITH A LARGE BOWL TO COMBINE YOUR INGREDIENTS. IN THE BOWL, MIX TOGETHER THE BEEF, ONIONS, MINCED GARLIC, MINCED ONIONS, STEAK SEASONING, WORCESTERSHIRE SAUCE, EGG, AND PEPPER UNTIL EVERYTHING IS WELL INCORPORATED. NEXT, TAKE A HANDFUL OF THE BEEF MIXTURE AND SHAPE IT INTO A PATTY. PLACE EACH PATTY ON A BAKING SHEET, CONTINUING UNTIL ALL THE MIXTURE IS UTILIZED. IN A SPACIOUS PAN SET OVER MEDIUM HEAT, ADD THE HAMBURGER STEAKS AND COOK FOR APPROXIMATELY 6 TO 7 MINUTES ON EACH SIDE. ONCE COOKED, REMOVE THE PATTIES FROM THE PAN AND SET THEM ASIDE.

NOW, LET'S MAKE THE GRAVY. IN A SEPARATE PAN ON MEDIUM HEAT, ADD OLIVE OIL AND FLOUR. STIR THE FLOUR CONTINUOUSLY AND COOK UNTIL IT REACHES YOUR DESIRED LEVEL OF BROWN. GRADUALLY POUR IN THE WATER, STIRRING UNTIL THE MIXTURE THICKENS. THEN, INCORPORATE THE BEEF BOUILLON AND PEPPER. FINALLY, RETURN THE BEEF PATTIES TO THE PAN, COVERING THEM WITH THE GRAVY. LOWER THE HEAT AND LET THE MIXTURE SIMMER FOR ABOUT 15 MINUTES. WHEN FINISHED, SERVE THIS DELIGHTFUL DISH ALONGSIDE MASHED POTATOES AND SAVOR THE FLAVORS!

CHICKEN FRIED CHICKEN

Prep Time 15 Minutes

Cooking Time 3 TO 4 Minutes

INGREDIENTS

2 chicken breasts
(cut down the middle
and cut in half)
all-purpose seasoning
garlic pepper Seasoning
Onion powder
Buttery steakhouse
(I use Kinder's)
1 egg
1 cup milk or buttermilk
2 cups flour

★★★★☆

The White Gravy
2 tablespoons butter
2 tablespoon oil
¼ cup flour
1 cup milk or more
(depends on how
thick you want your gravy)
Salt and pepper to taste
1 teaspoon buttery steak
house
(I use Kinder's)
1 teaspoon onion powder

DIRECTIONS 🍴 4

TO PREPARE THIS MOUTHWATERING CHICKEN FRIED CHICKEN, START BY LAYING A SHEET OF PARCHMENT PAPER ON YOUR COUNTERTOP. PLACE THE CHICKEN ON TOP OF THE PARCHMENT, THEN COVER IT WITH ANOTHER SHEET. USE A MEAT MALLET TO POUND THE CHICKEN UNTIL IT REACHES ABOUT ¼ INCH IN THICKNESS, THEN SET IT ASIDE IN A SMALL BOWL, COMBINE THE ALL-PURPOSE SEASONING, GARLIC PEPPER SEASONING, ONION POWDER, AND BUTTERY STEAKHOUSE SEASONING, MIXING WELL. SPRINKLE HALF OF THIS SEASONING BLEND GENEROUSLY OVER THE CHICKEN, THEN TRANSFER THE CHICKEN TO A LARGE BOWL. ADD THE EGG AND MILK TO THE BOWL, ENSURING THE CHICKEN IS WELL COATED IN ANOTHER LARGE BOWL, MIX THE FLOUR WITH THE REMAINING SEASONING. PREHEAT A SKILLET WITH OIL TO 350 DEGREES. DREDGE THE CHICKEN IN THE DRY BATTER, THEN CAREFULLY PLACE IT IN THE HOT OIL, COOKING FOR 3 TO 4 MINUTES ON EACH SIDE. ONCE COOKED, REMOVE THE CHICKEN AND PLACE IT ON A DRAINING RACK TO KEEP IT CRISPY.NEXT, POUR OFF ALL BUT ABOUT 2 TABLESPOONS OF THE OIL FROM THE SKILLET. ADD THE BUTTER AND FLOUR, COOKING THE MIXTURE UNTIL THE RAW FLOUR TASTE IS ELIMINATED, ABOUT 2 MINUTES. BE CAREFUL NOT TO LET IT BROWN. GRADUALLY ADD THE MILK WHILE STIRRING CONTINUOUSLY UNTIL THE MIXTURE THICKENS INTO GRAVY. FINALLY, STIR IN THE SALT AND PEPPER, ALONG WITH THE BUTTERY STEAKHOUSE SEASONING AND ONION POWDER.SERVE BY PLACING THE CHICKEN ON A PLATE AND GENEROUSLY POURING THE GRAVY OVER THE TOP. NOW, ENJOY YOUR DELICIOUS MEAL!

COUNTRY FRIED STEAK

 Prep Time 15 Minutes

 Cooking Time 25 Minutes

INGREDIENTS

8 cubed steaks

1 tablespoon

Canadian steak blend

1 tablespoon buttery

steakhouse

(I use Kinder's)

1 tablespoon garlic

powder

1 tablespoon onion

powder

1 tablespoon thyme

1 cup milk or buttermilk

1 cup milk or
buttermilk

2 eggs

2 cups flour

THE GRAVY

4 tbsp olive oil

1/2 chopped onion

1/4 cup flour

2 cups water

1 teaspoon salt

1 teaspoon pepper

1 teaspoon onion

OIL USED: CANOLA
OIL TEMP: 350 DEGREES
TOOLS: MEAT TENDERIZER

DIRECTIONS 4

TO CREATE A MOUTHWATERING COUNTRY FRIED STEAK, START BY LAYING A PIECE OF PARCHMENT PAPER ON THE COUNTERTOP AND PLACING YOUR STEAKS ON TOP. NEXT, COVER THE STEAKS WITH ANOTHER PIECE OF PARCHMENT PAPER. USING THE FLAT SIDE OF A MEAT TENDERIZER, GENTLY POUND THE STEAKS A FEW TIMES TO FLATTEN THEM. REMOVE THE TOP PARCHMENT PAPER AND SWITCH TO THE TEXTURED SIDE OF THE TENDERIZER TO TENDERIZE THE STEAKS FURTHER. IN A BOWL, COMBINE THE CANADIAN STEAK BLEND, BUTTERY STEAKHOUSE SEASONING, GARLIC POWDER, ONION POWDER, AND THYME, MIXING EVERYTHING TOGETHER. SEASON BOTH SIDES OF THE STEAKS WITH HALF OF THIS MIXTURE BEFORE SETTING THEM ASIDE. IN A SEPARATE BOWL, WHISK TOGETHER THE MILK AND EGGS UNTIL WELL COMBINED. ADD THE STEAKS INTO THE MILK AND EGG MIXTURE, ENSURING THEY ARE FULLY COATED. IN ANOTHER LARGE BOWL, MIX THE FLOUR WITH THE REMAINING SEASONING. HEAT OIL IN A LARGE SKILLET TO 350 DEGREES. ONCE THE OIL IS HOT, ADD THE STEAKS AND COOK FOR ABOUT 7 TO 8 MINUTES. ONCE COOKED, TRANSFER THEM TO A DRAINING RACK TO KEEP THEM CRISPY. IN A DIFFERENT SKILLET SET OVER MEDIUM HEAT, ADD OIL AND CHOPPED ONIONS. SAUTÉ THE ONIONS UNTIL THEY ARE TRANSLUCENT, THEN SPRINKLE IN THE FLOUR. COOK THE FLOUR UNTIL IT REACHES YOUR PREFERRED SHADE OF BROWN, THEN GRADUALLY ADD WATER, STIRRING UNTIL IT THICKENS INTO A GRAVY. SEASON WITH SALT, PEPPER, AND ONION POWDER. FINALLY, ADD THE STEAKS TO THE GRAVY, COVER, AND LET THEM SIMMER FOR ABOUT 15 MINUTES. SERVE WITH MASHED POTATOES OR RICE AND ENJOY!

GARLIC & HERB SALMON

 Prep Time 10 Minutes

 Cooking Time 25 Minutes

INGREDIENTS

4 salmon steaks

4 tablespoons olive oil

1 teaspoon creole seasoning

1 teaspoon buttery steakhouse

1 teaspoon onion powder

1 teaspoon garlic powder

1 teaspoon oregano

3 garlic cloves chopped

1 sprig of rosemary

4 tablespoons butter

DIRECTIONS 4

TO PREPARE THIS DELICIOUS SALMON DISH, START BY PLACING THE SALMON ON A CUTTING BOARD AND SETTING IT ASIDE. IN A BOWL, COMBINE THE CREOLE SEASONING, BUTTERY STEAKHOUSE SEASONING, ONION POWDER, GARLIC POWDER, AND OREGANO, MIXING THEM THOROUGHLY. DRIZZLE A BIT OF OLIVE OIL OVER EACH PIECE OF SALMON, THEN GENEROUSLY SPRINKLE THE SEASONING ON BOTH SIDES.

NEXT, HEAT TWO TABLESPOONS OF OLIVE OIL IN A LARGE SKILLET OVER MEDIUM HEAT. ONCE THE OIL IS HOT, ADD THE SALMON TO THE PAN. COOK THE SALMON FOR 4 TO 5 MINUTES BEFORE FLIPPING IT OVER. AFTER FLIPPING, COOK FOR AN ADDITIONAL 4 TO 5 MINUTES, THEN INCORPORATE 4 TABLESPOONS OF BUTTER. ONCE THE BUTTER HAS MELTED, ADD THE GARLIC AND ROSEMARY. USE A SPOON TO BASTE THE SALMON WITH THE GARLIC AND HERB BUTTER, GIVING IT A FLAVORFUL "BUTTER BATH."

REMOVE THE SKILLET FROM THE HEAT AND LET THE SALMON REST FOR 15 MINUTES, ALLOWING IT TO CONTINUE COOKING. BEFORE SERVING, GARNISH WITH PARSLEY AND A SQUEEZE OF FRESH LEMON JUICE, THEN ENJOY!

ITALIAN MEATBALL

 Prep Time 20 minutes

 Cooking Time
45 Minutes

INGREDIENTS

The Marinara
2 tablespoons olive oil
1 cup onions chopped
3 fresh garlic cloves chopped
1 can crushed tomatoes
1 can tomato sauce
½ teaspoon parsley
½ teaspoon Italian seasoning
½ teaspoon basil
½ teaspoon fennel seeds
½ teaspoon onion powder
½ teaspoon garlic powder
½ teaspoon sugar
½ teaspoon salt
½ teaspoon pepper

The Meatballs
1 lb. ground beef
½ onion chopped
2 tablespoons garlic chopped
1 tablespoon creole seasoning
½ teaspoon onion powder
½ teaspoon garlic powder
½ teaspoon paprika
½ teaspoon Italian seasoning
½ teaspoon basil
½ teaspoon fennel seeds
½ teaspoon oregano
1 teaspoon parsley
1 cup breadcrumbs
2 eggs
-Xtras-
6 sub rolls
Mozzarella cheese
Parmesan cheese
Parsley for garnish

★★★★☆

DIRECTIONS

🍴 6

TO PREPARE THESE MOUTHWATERING MEATBALL SUBS, START BY HEATING OLIVE OIL IN A LARGE SKILLET OVER MEDIUM HEAT AND ADDING CHOPPED ONIONS. SAUTÉ UNTIL THE ONIONS BECOME TRANSLUCENT, THEN INCORPORATE MINCED GARLIC AND COOK FOR AN ADDITIONAL MINUTE. NEXT, MIX IN CRUSHED TOMATOES, TOMATO SAUCE, PARSLEY, ITALIAN SEASONING, BASIL, FENNEL SEEDS, ONION POWDER, GARLIC POWDER, SUGAR, SALT, AND PEPPER. STIR WELL, ADD WATER, AND LET THE MIXTURE SIMMER FOR 25 TO 30 MINUTES BEFORE REMOVING IT FROM HEAT AND SETTING IT ASIDE. IN A SEPARATE LARGE BOWL, COMBINE GROUND BEEF, CHOPPED ONIONS, MINCED GARLIC, CREOLE SEASONING, ONION POWDER, GARLIC POWDER, PAPRIKA, ITALIAN SEASONING, BASIL, FENNEL SEEDS, OREGANO, PARSLEY, BREADCRUMBS, EGGS, AND PARMESAN CHEESE. MIX ALL THE INGREDIENTS THOROUGHLY. USING A SCOOP, SHAPE THE MIXTURE INTO MEATBALLS, ROLLING THEM IN YOUR HANDS UNTIL THEY'RE COMPLETE. IN A LARGE POT OR DEEP FRYER PREHEAT OIL TO 350 DEGREES FAHRENHEIT AND CAREFULLY DROP THE MEATBALLS INTO THE HOT OIL, ENSURING NOT TO OVERCROWD THE POT. FRY THEM FOR ABOUT 3 TO 4 MINUTES UNTIL THEY DEVELOP A GOLDEN CRUST AND ARE NICELY BROWNED. ONCE COOKED, TRANSFER THE MEATBALLS TO THE MARINARA SAUCE AND ALLOW THEM TO SIMMER FOR APPROXIMATELY 25 MINUTES. MEANWHILE, ARRANGE SUB ROLLS ON A BAKING SHEET AND FILL THEM GENEROUSLY WITH MEATBALLS. DRIZZLE SOME MARINARA SAUCE ON TOP, SPRINKLE WITH CHEESE, AND GARNISH WITH PARSLEY. BAKE IN A PREHEATED OVEN AT 400 DEGREES UNTIL THE CHEESE MELTS AND THE BREAD IS TOASTED. ONCE FINISHED, REMOVE FROM THE OVEN AND ENJOY YOUR DELICIOUS CREATION!

ORANGE CHICKEN

 Prep Time 15 Minutes

 Cooking Time 20 Minutes

INGREDIENTS

3 chicken breast or
chicken thighs

3 egg whites

1/3 cup corn starch

1/3 cup flour

1 tablespoon salt

2 tablespoons sesame
oil

3 garlic cloves minced

1/4 cup soy sauce

2 tablespoons rice
vinegar

2 tablespoons rice vinegar
1 cup orange juice
1 tablespoons ginger paste
1/3 cup white sugar
1/3 cup brown sugar
Corn Starch Slurry
1 tablespoon cornstarch
2 tablespoons water
1 tablespoon orange zest
(green onions for garnish)

DIRECTIONS 4

TO PREPARE THIS DELIGHTFUL ORANGE CHICKEN, START BY COMBINING THE CHICKEN, SALT, EGG WHITES, CORNSTARCH, AND FLOUR IN A LARGE BOWL, MIXING EVERYTHING THOROUGHLY. IN A LARGE POT, HEAT OIL TO 350 DEGREES. ONCE THE OIL IS HOT, ADD THE CHICKEN PIECES ONE AT A TIME, BEING CAREFUL NOT TO OVERCROWD THE POT. FRY THE CHICKEN FOR APPROXIMATELY 10 MINUTES UNTIL IT TURNS GOLDEN BROWN. REMOVE IT FROM THE POT AND PLACE IT ON A DRAINING RACK TO KEEP IT CRISPY.

IN A SEPARATE LARGE SKILLET OR WOK SET TO MEDIUM HEAT, ADD SESAME OIL, GARLIC, SOY SAUCE, RICE VINEGAR, ORANGE JUICE, GINGER PASTE, WHITE SUGAR, AND BROWN SUGAR. STIR WELL TO COMBINE. WHEN THE SUGARS HAVE MELTED AND FORMED A COHESIVE MIXTURE, POUR IN THE CORNSTARCH SLURRY AND STIR UNTIL THE SAUCE THICKENS. THEN, ADD THE COOKED CHICKEN TO THE SKILLET. FINISH BY SPRINKLING ORANGE ZEST OVER THE TOP AND MIXING EVERYTHING TOGETHER TO ENSURE THE CHICKEN IS WELL-COATED. GARNISH WITH GREEN ONIONS, SERVE, AND ENJOY!

ROASTED AIRFRYER/OVEN CHICKEN

 Prep Time 20 Minutes

 Cooking Time 55 Minutes

INGREDIENTS

2 to 4 pound chicken

1 cup cajun injection

creole butter

1 tablespoon thyme

1 tablespoon rosemary

1 tablespoon olive oil

1 tablespoon garlic paste

2 tablespoon creole

butter

DIRECTIONS 4

BEGIN BY TAKING OUT THE INNER BAG FROM THE CHICKEN. CLEAN THE CHICKEN THOROUGHLY, THEN USE A PAPER TOWEL TO PAT IT DRY. PLACE THE CHICKEN ON A BAKING SHEET. INJECT CAJUN CREOLE BUTTER INTO THE CHICKEN, ENSURING TO TARGET THE LEGS, THIGHS, AND WINGS, AND MAKE SEVERAL INJECTIONS IN THE BREAST AS WELL. IN A SMALL BOWL, COMBINE THYME, ROSEMARY, OLIVE OIL, GARLIC PASTE, AND CREOLE BUTTER. RUB THIS MIXTURE GENEROUSLY OVER THE CHICKEN'S EXTERIOR, ENSURING IT'S WELL COATED. COOK THE CHICKEN UNCOVERED IN THE AIR FRYER OR OVEN AT 375 DEGREES FOR 45 TO 55 MINUTES, OR UNTIL IT'S GOLDEN BROWN AND THE JUICES RUN CLEAR. THE INTERNAL TEMPERATURE SHOULD REACH 165 DEGREES. ONCE DONE, REMOVE THE CHICKEN AND COVER IT WITH FOIL. ALLOW IT TO REST FOR 15 MINUTES BEFORE ENJOYING.

★★★★☆

SAUSAGE & PEPPERS

 Prep Time 15 Minutes

 Cooking Time 20 Minutes

INGREDIENTS

2 packs of polish sausage

1 green bell pepper sliced

1 red bell pepper sliced

1 yellow bell pepper sliced

1 onion sliced

1 cup BBQ sauce

8 hot dog buns

★★★★☆

DIRECTIONS 8

TO PREPARE THESE TASTY SAUSAGE, PEPPERS AND ONIONS, START BY SLICING THE SAUSAGES LENGTHWISE LIKE A HOT DOG BUN, THEN CUT EACH SAUSAGE DOWN THE CENTER. PREHEAT A LARGE SKILLET OVER MEDIUM HEAT. ONCE IT'S HOT, ADD THE SAUSAGES AND COOK UNTIL THEY'RE BROWNED ON ALL SIDES. REMOVE THE SAUSAGES FROM THE PAN AND SET THEM ASIDE. IN THE SAME SKILLET, ADD THE BELL PEPPERS AND ONIONS, SAUTÉING UNTIL THEY BECOME TENDER. NEXT, RETURN THE SAUSAGES TO THE PAN AND POUR IN THE BBQ SAUCE. ALLOW EVERYTHING TO COOK TOGETHER FOR ABOUT FIVE MINUTES, LETTING THE FLAVORS BLEND. ONCE READY, PLACE THE SAUSAGE AND PEPPERS ONTO YOUR BUN AND DRIZZLE WITH ADDITIONAL BBQ SAUCE FROM THE SKILLET. ENJOY YOUR DELICIOUS CREATION!

SEAFOOD GUMBO

 Prep Time 15 Minutes

 Cooking Time 1 Hour 25 Minutes

INGREDIENTS

1 pack of andouille
sausage cut into chunks
1/2 cup vegetable oil
1/2 cup butter
1 cup flour
1 cup sweet onion
1 cup green bell pepper
1 cup red bell peppers
1 cup yellow bell
peppers
1 cup celery
1 cup green onion
4 cloves fresh garlic
chopped

6 cups seafood stock
1 cup beer
1 tablespoon old bay
1 teaspoon creole seasoning
1 teaspoon onion powder
1 teaspoon garlic powder
1 teaspoon thyme
1 teaspoon gumbo file
2 bay leaves
1 lb. peeled and deveined
shrimp
8oz crab meat
2 cups fresh okra chunks
1 tablespoon parsley

DIRECTIONS 4

TO PREPARE THIS DELECTABLE SEAFOOD GUMBO, BEGIN BY TAKING A LARGE POT AND SETTING IT OVER MEDIUM HEAT. ADD THE SAUSAGE AND COOK UNTIL IT'S NICELY BROWNED, WHICH SHOULD TAKE ABOUT 5 MINUTES. ONCE DONE, REMOVE THE SAUSAGE AND SET IT ASIDE. IN THE SAME POT, INCORPORATE THE VEGETABLE OILS, BUTTER, AND FLOUR, STIRRING CONTINUOUSLY UNTIL THE MIXTURE ACHIEVES A COCOA BROWN COLOR. THIS PROCESS WILL TAKE AROUND 20 MINUTES, SO BE PATIENT. ONCE YOU'VE REACHED YOUR DESIRED SHADE OF BROWN, ADD IN ALL THE VEGETABLES AND GARLIC, COOKING UNTIL THE VEGGIES BECOME TENDER. NEXT, POUR IN THE SEAFOOD STOCK AND BEER, ALLOWING IT TO COME TO A BOIL BEFORE ADDING ALL THE SEASONINGS. LET THE FLAVORS MELD FOR ABOUT 10 MINUTES, THEN INTRODUCE THE SAUSAGE, SHRIMP, CRAB MEAT, AND OKRA INTO THE POT. REDUCE THE HEAT AND LET IT SIMMER FOR ANOTHER 15 MINUTES.REMOVE THE BAY LEAVES AND FINALLY, SERVE THE GUMBO AND GARNISH WITH SOME PARSLEY FOR A BEAUTIFUL PRESENTATION. DON'T FORGET TO PAIR IT WITH RICE AND ENJOY!

SHEPHERD'S PIE

 Prep Time 20 minutes

 Cooking Time
1 hour 30 MINUTES

4

INGREDIENTS

5lbs. russet potatoes

1 tablespoon salt

1 stick Kerrygold garlic
and herb butter

1/2 cup sour cream

1 tablespoon Kinder's buttery
steakhouse

1 1/2 to 2 cups heavy cream or milk

3 lbs. ground beef

1 medium onion chopped

1 tablespoon Kinder's caramelize
onion butter

1 tablespoon Kinder's brown
butter roasted garlic

1 teaspoon red pepper flakes

2 cloves garlic chopped

1 tablespoon tomato paste

1 1/2 frozen peas and carrots

1 cup frozen corn

1/4 cup red wine (I use cooking wine)

3 tablespoon Worcestershire sauce

1 tablespoon rosemary

1 tablespoon thyme

2 tablespoons flour

1 cup beef broth

Pepper to taste

1 cup coby Jack cheese

1 cup cheddar

1 tablespoon parsley

DIRECTIONS

TO PREPARE SHEPHERD'S PIE, BEGIN BY CREATING THE MASHED POTATO TOPPING. PEEL AND DICE THE POTATOES, THEN RINSE THEM IN A BOWL. PLACE THE POTATOES IN A POT OF WATER OVER MEDIUM HEAT AND ADD SALT. COOK UNTIL TENDER FOR ABOUT 12 MINUTES, THEN DRAIN THE WATER. RETURN THE POTATOES TO THE POT AND MIX IN KERRYGOLD GARLIC AND HERB BUTTER, SOUR CREAM, KINDER'S BUTTERY STEAKHOUSE, AND HEAVY CREAM. MASH THE POTATOES UNTIL SMOOTH USING A POTATO MASHER OR HAND MIXER. COVER THE POTATOES AND SET ASIDE. IN A CAST IRON PAN, COOK THE GROUND BEEF UNTIL BROWN. DRAIN THE GREASE AND RETURN THE BEEF TO THE PAN. ADD ONIONS AND COOK UNTIL TRANSLUCENT. MIX IN KENDER'S CARAMELIZED ONION BUTTER, BROWN BUTTER ROASTED GARLIC, RED PEPPER FLAKES, AND GARLIC. COOK UNTIL THE GARLIC IS FRAGRANT, THEN ADD TOMATO PASTE. COOK FOR ANOTHER 2 MINUTES, THEN ADD FROZEN PEAS, CARROTS, CORN, RED WINE, WORCESTERSHIRE SAUCE, THYME, ROSEMARY, FLOUR, BEEF BROTH, AND PEPPER. STIR WELL, COVER, AND SIMMER ON MEDIUM-LOW FOR 25 MINUTES. REMOVE THE LID AND TOP WITH CHEESE FOLLOWED BY THE MASHED POTATOES. SPRINKLE WITH PARSLEY THEN PLACE THE BAKING DISH ON A RIMMED BAKING SHEET TO PREVENT SPILLS. BAKE UNCOVERED IN A 375 DEGREES OVEN FOR 25-30 MINUTES. ALLOW TO COOL FOR 15 MINUTES BEFORE SERVING. ENJOY YOUR MEAL!

★★★★☆

STUFFED CABBAGE ROLLS

 Prep Time 20 Minutes

 Cooking Time 1 Hour

INGREDIENTS

1 whole cabbage

6 cups water

1 tablespoon salt

1 onion chopped

1 cup mushrooms

3 cloves fresh Garlic

1lb ground beef

1 teaspoon salt

1 teaspoon pepper

1 teaspoon onion powder

1 teaspoon garlic powder

1 teaspoon creole seasoning

½ cup jasmine rice

DIRECTIONS 6

TO PREPARE THESE TASTY CABBAGE ROLLS, START BY FILLING A LARGE POT WITH WATER AND SETTING IT TO MEDIUM HEAT. ADD THE CABBAGE AND SOME SALT. COVER THE POT AND BOIL THE CABBAGE UNTIL THE OUTER LEAVES CAN BE EASILY PULLED AWAY FROM THE HEAD. ONCE DONE, REMOVE THE LEAVES AND SET THEM ASIDE.

IN A LARGE SKILLET ON MEDIUM HEAT, POUR IN THE OLIVE OIL AND SAUTÉ THE ONIONS, MUSHROOMS, AND GARLIC. AFTER COOKING, REMOVE THIS MIXTURE FROM THE SKILLET AND SET IT ASIDE. IN THE SAME SKILLET, ADD THE GROUND BEEF ALONG WITH SALT, PEPPER, ONION POWDER, GARLIC POWDER, AND CREOLE SEASONING. COOK THE BEEF UNTIL IT'S FULLY BROWNED, THEN MIX IN THE MUSHROOM AND ONION MIXTURE ALONG WITH CRUSHED TOMATOES, ENSURING EVERYTHING IS WELL COMBINED. FINALLY, STIR IN THE UNCOOKED RICE AND REMOVE THE SKILLET FROM THE HEAT.

TAKE ONE CABBAGE LEAF AT A TIME AND PLACE SOME FILLING INSIDE. ROLL IT UP LIKE A BURRITO, MAKING SURE TO TUCK IN THE CORNERS. ARRANGE THE ROLLED CABBAGE LEAVES SIDE BY SIDE IN A BAKING DISH. REPEAT THIS PROCESS UNTIL ALL THE FILLING IS USED. POUR CHICKEN BROTH OVER THE CABBAGE ROLLS, THEN TOP WITH THE REMAINING CRUSHED TOMATOES, SPRINKLING WITH ADDITIONAL SALT AND PEPPER. USE LEFTOVER CABBAGE LEAVES TO COVER THE ROLLS BEFORE PLACING THE DISH IN A 350°F OVEN FOR ABOUT AN HOUR.

AFTER BAKING, REMOVE THE DISH FROM THE OVEN AND DISCARD THE CABBAGE LEAVES ON TOP. ALLOW THE ROLLS TO REST FOR AT LEAST 30 MINUTES BEFORE SERVING. WHILE THEY CAN BE ENJOYED RIGHT AWAY, THEY ARE EVEN BETTER THE NEXT DAY.

75

SWEET AND SOUR CHICKEN

 Prep Time
15 Minutes

Cooking Time
30 Minutes

INGREDIENTS

2 chicken breast cut into chunks

1 teaspoon salt

1 teaspoon white pepper

1 tablespoon cornstarch

1 teaspoon baking powder

1/2 teaspoon salt

1 egg

1/4 cup cold water

1/2 cup ketchup

1/2 cup sugar

2 tablespoons rice vinegar

1 teaspoon dark soy sauce

1 tablespoon sesame oil

1 onion chopped

1 bell pepper chopped

1 red bell pepper chopped

1 clove garlic chopped

1 20oz can pineapple tidbits

(reserve the tidbits)

DIRECTIONS 4

TO CREATE THIS DELIGHTFUL SWEET AND SOUR CHICKEN, START BY PLACING THE CHICKEN BREAST IN A MEDIUM BOWL AND SEASONING IT WITH SALT AND PEPPER. IN A SEPARATE BOWL, COMBINE FLOUR, CORNSTARCH, BAKING POWDER, SALT, EGG WHITE, AND COLD WATER. IN ANOTHER BOWL, MIX KETCHUP, SUGAR, RICE VINEGAR, AND DARK SOY SAUCE THOROUGHLY. DRAIN THE JUICE FROM THE PINEAPPLE TIDBITS AND INCORPORATE 1/4 CUP IT INTO THE RED SAUCE (THE KETCHUP AND SUGAR MIXTURE), SETTING ASIDE THE TIDBITS.

IN A LARGE POT, HEAT COOKING OIL TO 350 DEGREES. ONCE THE OIL IS HOT, DIP THE CHICKEN INTO THE WET FLOUR BATTER ONE PIECE AT A TIME, THEN CAREFULLY DROP IT INTO THE OIL, ENSURING NOT TO OVERCROWD THE POT. FRY FOR ABOUT 4 TO 5 MINUTES UNTIL GOLDEN BROWN, REPEATING THE PROCESS UNTIL ALL THE CHICKEN IS COOKED. INCREASE THE TEMPERATURE TO 375 DEGREES, THEN RETURN THE CHICKEN TO THE POT FOR AN ADDITIONAL 2 TO 3 MINUTES TO ACHIEVE EXTRA CRISPINESS AND ENSURE IT HOLDS UP AGAINST THE SAUCE. REMOVE THE CHICKEN AND PLACE IT ON A DRAINING RACK.

IN A LARGE SKILLET SET OVER MEDIUM HEAT, ADD SESAME OIL. WHEN HEATED, TOSS IN THE ONIONS, BELL PEPPERS, AND RED PEPPERS, COOKING UNTIL TENDER FOR ABOUT 2 MINUTES. THEN, ADD THE GARLIC AND SAUTÉ UNTIL FRAGRANT, ABOUT ONE MINUTE. STIR IN THE PINEAPPLE TIDBITS, MIX WELL, AND THEN ADD THE CHICKEN, POURING THE SAUCE OVER THE TOP. COMBINE EVERYTHING THOROUGHLY AND SERVE OVER A BED OF RICE. ENJOY YOUR MEAL!

SHORT RIBS

 Prep Time 20 minutes

 Cooking Time
45 Minutes to 2 hours

🍴 4

INGREDIENTS

6 to 8 short ribs

2 tablespoons olive oil

1 tablespoon steak king

1 tablespoon garlic powder

1 tablespoon onion powder

1 creole seasoning

1 tablespoon Braggs 24

herbs and spices

1 green bell pepper

1 red bell pepper

1 whole onion

3 cloves garlic

1 tablespoon black pepper

1 tablespoon tomato paste

32oz beef broth

1 chicken bouillon packet

1/4 cup red cooking wine

1 sprig thyme

1 sprig rosemary

2 bay leaves cornstarch slurry

1 tablespoon cornstarch

2 tablespoons water

DIRECTIONS

TO MAKE BRAISED SHORT RIBS, PLACE THE SHORT RIBS IN A LARGE BOWL AND ADD IN OLIVE OIL, STEAK KING STEAK SEASONING, GARLIC POWDER, ONION POWDER, CREOLE SEASONING, AND BRAGGS 24 HERBS AND SPICES. RUB ALL OF THE SEASONING INTO THE SHORT RIBS. NEXT, IN A LARGE PAN OR POT, ADD IN 2 TABLESPOONS OF OLIVE OIL AND SEAR THE SHORT RIBS ON ALL SIDES. ONCE SEARED, REMOVE THEM FROM THE PAN AND PLACE THEM IN A DUTCH OVEN OR NINJA PRESSURE COOKER. IN THE SAME PAN, ADD IN BELL PEPPERS, RED PEPPERS, ONION, GARLIC, BLACK PEPPER, TOMATO PASTE, BEEF BROTH, BEEF BOUILLON PACKET, RED COOKING WINE, THYME, ROSEMARY, AND BAY LEAVES. PLACE THE TOP ON THE DUTCH OVEN OR PRESSURE COOKER AND SET THE PRESSURE COOKER TO HIGH FOR 45 MINUTES. IF USING A DUTCH OVEN, SET THE OVEN TO 350 DEGREES AND COOK FOR 2 HOURS. ONCE DONE, REMOVE FROM THE OVEN AND ADD TWO CUPS OF THE BROTH TO A SMALL POT SET TO MEDIUM HEAT. MAKE A CORNSTARCH SLURRY BY ADDING THE CORNSTARCH AND WATER TOGETHER. THEN ADD IT TO THE POT, COOKING UNTIL IT THICKENS INTO A GRAVY. POUR THE GRAVY OVER THE SHORT RIBS AND SERVE WITH MASHED POTATOES AND VEGGIES FOR A DELICIOUS AND HEARTY MEAL

★★★★☆

SMOTHERED PORK CHOPS

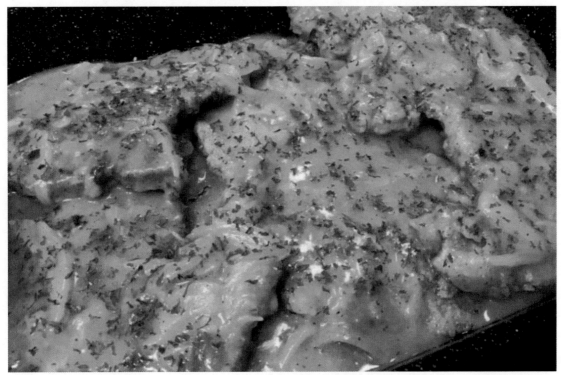

 Prep Time 15 Minutes

 Cooking Time 20 Minutes

INGREDIENTS

4 to 6 center cut pork chops

1 teaspoon salt

1 teaspoon pepper

1 teaspoon creole

1 teaspoon garlic powder

1 teaspoon onion powder

1 teaspoon paprika

1 teaspoon thyme

1 teaspoon rosemary

2 cups flour

The Gravy

1 cup chopped onions

¼ cups flour

½ teaspoon onion powder

½ teaspoon garlic powder

½ teaspoon Creole seasoning

½ teaspoon thyme

½ teaspoon rosemary

1 teaspoon browning seasoning

2 cups chicken broth

DIRECTIONS 4

TO CREATE THESE MOUTHWATERING SMOTHERED PORK CHOPS, START BY MIXING TOGETHER SALT, PEPPER, CREOLE SEASONING, GARLIC POWDER, ONION POWDER, PAPRIKA, THYME, AND ROSEMARY IN A SMALL BOWL. USE HALF OF THIS SEASONING MIX TO SEASON BOTH SIDES OF YOUR PORK CHOPS, THEN SET THEM ASIDE. IN A SEPARATE LARGE BOWL, COMBINE FLOUR WITH THE REMAINING SEASONING AND SET IT ASIDE AS WELL.

NEXT, HEAT OIL IN A LARGE SKILLET OVER MEDIUM HEAT UNTIL IT REACHES 350 DEGREES. DREDGE THE SEASONED PORK CHOPS IN THE FLOUR MIXTURE AND CAREFULLY PLACE THEM INTO THE HOT OIL. COOK UNTIL EACH SIDE IS GOLDEN BROWN, WHICH SHOULD TAKE ABOUT 7 MINUTES. ONCE COOKED, REMOVE THE PORK CHOPS FROM THE PAN.

IN THE SAME SKILLET, ADD ONIONS AND SAUTÉ UNTIL THEY BECOME TENDER. THEN, SPRINKLE IN THE FLOUR AND STIR UNTIL IT STARTS TO BROWN. ADD THE ONION POWDER, GARLIC POWDER, CREOLE SEASONING, THYME, AND ROSEMARY, MIXING EVERYTHING TOGETHER. INCORPORATE THE BROWNING SEASONING, FOLLOWED BY THE CHICKEN BROTH. STIR CONTINUOUSLY UNTIL THE MIXTURE THICKENS INTO GRAVY.

ONCE THE GRAVY HAS THICKENED, RETURN THE PORK CHOPS TO THE SKILLET, ENSURING THEY ARE COVERED IN GRAVY. ALLOW EVERYTHING TO SIMMER FOR ABOUT 15 MINUTES UNTIL THE PORK CHOPS BECOME TENDER. FINISH BY GARNISHING WITH PARSLEY. SERVE ALONGSIDE STEAMED RICE OR POTATOES, AND ENJOY!

SOUTHERN FRIED CHICKEN

 Prep Time 20 minutes

 Cooking Time
25 Minutes

4

INGREDIENTS

8-piece chicken of your choice

1 tablespoon Creole Seasoning

1 tablespoon roasted garlic powder

1 tablespoon onion powder

1 tablespoon paprika

¼ cup all-purpose Flour

2 cups water

The Dry Batter

4 cups all purpose

¼ cup cornstarch

1 tablespoon Creole seasoning

1 tablespoon roasted garlic powder

1 tablespoon onion powder

1 tablespoon paprika

★★★★☆

DIRECTIONS

TO PREPARE THIS MOUTHWATERING SOUTHERN FRIED CHICKEN, BEGIN WITH THE WET BATTER. IN A LARGE BOWL, COMBINE THE CREOLE SEASONING, ROASTED GARLIC, ONION POWDER, PAPRIKA, ALL-PURPOSE FLOUR, AND WATER, THEN MIX THOROUGHLY. THE BATTER SHOULD BE SLIGHTLY THINNER THAN PANCAKE BATTER. NEXT, ADD YOUR CHICKEN PIECES AND COAT THEM WELL.

NOW, FOR THE DRY MIXTURE, TAKE ANOTHER LARGE BOWL AND COMBINE ALL THE INGREDIENTS FOR THE DRY BATTER, MIXING THEM WELL. HEAT OIL TO 365 DEGREES. ONCE THE OIL REACHES THE PERFECT TEMPERATURE, TAKE EACH PIECE OF WET-BATTERED CHICKEN AND GENTLY DIP IT INTO THE DRY BATTER FOR AN EVEN COAT. ENSURE IT'S WELL-COATED BEFORE PLACING IT INTO THE HOT OIL.

AVOID OVERCROWDING THE POT AND DON'T PLACE THE PIECES TOO CLOSE TOGETHER. REFRAIN FROM STIRRING THE CHICKEN UNTIL THE CRUST HAS SET. COOK THE CHICKEN FOR 25 MINUTES, THEN REMOVE IT AND PLACE IT ON A DRAINING RACK TO MAINTAIN ITS CRISPINESS. FINISH IT OFF WITH SOME CLASSIC HOT SAUCE AND ENJOY!

KELLZ REFLECTION

As a young girl, I fondly remember the countless hours spent in the kitchen with my mother, a place filled with laughter, warmth, and the tantalizing aroma of home-cooked meals. I loved watching my mom skillfully prepare wonderful dishes, each one a masterpiece in its own right. The clinking of pots and pans, the sizzle of ingredients hitting the hot pan, and the delightful chatter between us made those moments magical. My mother's hands moved with such grace and confidence, turning simple ingredients into delicious feasts. These cherished memories of cooking together not only taught me the art of making food but also the joy of sharing love through every meal.

SIDE DISHES

BROCCOLI CASSEROLE

 Prep Time 30 Minutes

 Cooking Time 45 Hours

INGREDIENTS

4 cups white rice
(I use 2 success boil in a
bag rice) Follow package
instructions.

12 ounces of broccoli

½ stick butter

½ of a large onion diced

1 teaspoon garlic paste.

1 teaspoon garlic
powder

1 teaspoon onion
powder

4 oz Coby Jack cheese
(shredded)

4 os Monterey Jack
Cheese (shredded)
4 oz sharp cheddar
cheese(shredded)
½ cup sour cream
½ can of cream of chicken
and mushroom soup
1 can broccoli and
cheddar soup
1 cup milk
1 tablespoon parsley

9x13 Inch

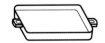

DIRECTIONS 6

COOK BOIL-IN-THE-BAG RICE ACCORDING TO THE INSTRUCTIONS ON THE BOX, OR YOU CAN USE ANY RICE YOU PREFER. THIS RECIPE REQUIRES 2 CUPS OF RICE, REGARDLESS OF THE TYPE, AS LONG AS THE TOTAL IS 4 CUPS. IN A SEPARATE POT, BRING APPROXIMATELY 4 CUPS OF WATER OR CHICKEN BROTH (FOR EXTRA FLAVOR) TO A BOIL AND ADD THE BROCCOLI. COOK THE BROCCOLI UNTIL IT'S TENDER, WHICH SHOULD TAKE ABOUT 3 MINUTES. ONCE DONE, REMOVE THE BROCCOLI AND PLACE IT ON A PAPER TOWEL. DISCARD THE BROCCOLI WATER AND RETURN THE POT TO THE STOVE OVER MEDIUM HEAT.ADD BUTTER AND ONIONS TO THE PAN, SAUTÉING THE ONIONS UNTIL THEY BECOME TRANSLUCENT. THEN, MIX IN GARLIC PASTE, GARLIC POWDER, AND ONION POWDER. RETURN THE BROCCOLI TO THE PAN, USING A SPATULA TO CHOP IT TO YOUR DESIRED CONSISTENCY. LOWER THE HEAT TO A SIMMER AND INCORPORATE SOUR CREAM, RICE, CREAM OF CHICKEN AND MUSHROOM SOUP, BROCCOLI AND CHEDDAR SOUP, HALF OF THE COLBY AND MONTEREY JACK CHEESE, SHARP CHEDDAR CHEESE, AND MILK. STIR EVERYTHING THOROUGHLY UNTIL THE CHEESE MELTS.
POUR THE MIXTURE INTO A CASSEROLE DISH AND TOP IT WITH THE REMAINING CHEESES. BAKE AT 350 DEGREES FOR APPROXIMATELY 45 MINUTES, OR UNTIL IT TURNS GOLDEN BROWN. ONCE FINISHED, LET IT SIT FOR 15 MINUTES BEFORE SERVING. ENJOY!

BUTTER BEANS

 Prep Time 8
Hours

 Cooking Time
2 Hours

INGREDIENTS

1 pound bag lima beans

2 smoked neck bones

1 tablespoon chicken

Better Than Bouillon

½ onion chopped

1 tablespoon roasted garlic powder

1 tablespoon sugar

Salt and pepper to taste

½ stick or 4 tablespoons butter

DIRECTIONS 6

TO MAKE BUTTERBEANS, START BY ADDING THEM TO A LARGE BOWL OF WATER AND LET THEM SOAK FOR 8 HOURS. ONCE THEY HAVE SOAKED, TRANSFER THEM TO A LARGE POT SET TO MEDIUM HEAT AND COVER BEANS WITH ABOUT 1/2 INCH OF WATER. LET THE BEANS COOK UNTIL THEY START TO COME TOGETHER. THEN, ADD IN CHOPPED ONIONS, BETTER THAN BOUILLON, SUGAR, SALT, PEPPER, AND BUTTER. COVER THE POT AND CONTINUE TO COOK ON MEDIUM-LOW HEAT UNTIL THE BEANS ARE TENDER, WHICH SHOULD TAKE ABOUT 2 HOURS. SERVE WITH A SIDE OF CORN BREAD FOR A DELICIOUS AND HEARTY MEAL.

GREEN BEANS WITH GARLIC AND LEMON

 Prep Time
5 Minutes

 Cooking Time
15 Minutes

INGREDIENTS

8 oz green beans
trimmed
2 cloves fresh garlic
2 tablespoons butter
Juice from ½ of a fresh
lemon
Salt and pepper

★★★★☆

DIRECTIONS 2

TO CREATE THESE TASTY GREEN BEANS, BEGIN BY BOILING A LARGE POT OF WATER. ONCE BOILING, ADD THE GREEN BEANS AND COOK THEM FOR AROUND FOUR MINUTES BEFORE DRAINING. IN A MEDIUM SKILLET, MELT THE BUTTER AND THEN ADD THE GARLIC. LET THE GARLIC INFUSE INTO THE BUTTER, THEN ADD THE GREEN BEANS, TOSSING THEM FOR ABOUT A MINUTE BEFORE SQUEEZING IN SOME LEMON JUICE AND ADDING THE SALT AND PEPPER. REMOVE FROM HEAT AND ENJOY YOUR DELIGHTFUL DISH!

ROSEMARY GARLIC ASPARAGUS

 Prep Time
5 Minutes

 Cooking Time
10 Hours

INGREDIENTS

1/2 pound fresh asparagus

2 tablespoons butter

1 clove garlic chopped

1 sprig rosemary

salt and pepper to taste

squeeze fresh lemon juice

★★★★☆

DIRECTIONS 2

TO PREPARE THIS DELICIOUS ASPARAGUS, START BY TRIMMING OFF THE WOODY ENDS. IN A STEAMING POT FILLED WITH 1 CUP OF WATER, ADD THE ASPARAGUS AND STEAM FOR 4 TO 5 MINUTES, OR UNTIL FORK-TENDER. ONCE DONE, REMOVE AND SET ASIDE. IN A SKILLET OVER MEDIUM HEAT, MELT THE BUTTER. WHEN THE BUTTER IS MELTED, ADD THE GARLIC AND ROSEMARY, COOKING FOR ABOUT A MINUTE UNTIL FRAGRANT. NEXT, INCORPORATE THE ASPARAGUS AND SAUTÉ FOR ABOUT 2 MINUTES TO MELD THE FLAVORS. REMOVE THE ROSEMARY SPRIG, SQUEEZE SOME LEMON FOR A FRESH TOUCH, AND ENJOY!

SOUTHERN FRIED CORN

 Prep Time
15 Minutes

 Cooking Time
15 Minutes

INGREDIENTS

14 to 16 ears of fresh corn

shucked and cut from the cob

2 tablespoon bacon grease

½ stick or ¼ cup butter

¼ cup sugar

1 cup heavy cream

1 teaspoon salt

1 teaspoon pepper

Corn starch slurry

Corn Starch Slurry

1 tablespoon cornstarch

2 tablespoons water

DIRECTIONS 6

TO PREPARE THIS DELECTABLE CREAM-STYLE CORN, BEGIN BY HEATING YOUR BACON GREASE IN A SKILLET OVER MEDIUM HEAT. ONCE THE GREASE IS WARMED, ADD THE BUTTER AND ALLOW IT TO MELT COMPLETELY. NEXT, INCORPORATE THE CORN AND COOK FOR APPROXIMATELY 15 MINUTES. AFTER THAT, STIR IN THE SUGAR, HEAVY CREAM, SALT, AND PEPPER. FINALLY, ADD THE CORNSTARCH SLURRY, WHICH IS SIMPLY A MIX OF CORNSTARCH AND WATER, AND STIR UNTIL THE CORN THICKENS. SERVE IT ALONGSIDE SOME FRESH TOMATOES AND HOMEMADE BISCUITS FOR A DELIGHTFUL MEAL!

SOUTHERN FRIED OKRA

Prep Time 10 minutes

Cooking Time
3 to 4 Minutes

🍴 4

INGREDIENTS

18 fresh okra pods, sliced

1/3 inch thick

2 eggs

1 cup buttermilk

2 cups corn meal

½ cup flour

1 teaspoon creole seasoning

1 teaspoon onion powder

1 teaspoon garlic powder

½ teaspoon salt

1 teaspoon pepper

DIRECTIONS

TO PREPARE THIS TASTY FRIED OKRA, START BY COMBINING THE EGGS AND BUTTERMILK IN A LARGE BOWL, THEN ADD THE OKRA AND MIX WELL BEFORE SETTING IT ASIDE. IN ANOTHER LARGE BOWL, COMBINE THE CORNMEAL, FLOUR, CREOLE SEASONING, GARLIC POWDER, SALT, AND PEPPER, MIXING THOROUGHLY. HEAT OIL IN A LARGE POT OR DEEP FRYER TO 350 DEGREES. WHILE THE OIL HEATS, COAT THE OKRA IN THE DRY MIXTURE AND PLACE THEM ON A BAKING SHEET. ONCE THE OIL REACHES THE TARGET TEMPERATURE, CAREFULLY DROP THE OKRA INTO THE FRYER. FRY IN BATCHES UNTIL THE OKRA TURNS GOLDEN BROWN, WHICH SHOULD TAKE ABOUT 2 TO 3 MINUTES. REMOVE THE OKRA AND LET IT DRAIN ON A RACK. SPRINKLE A LITTLE SALT RIGHT AFTER FRYING AND ENJOY!

TERIYAKI BRUSSEL SPROUTS

 Prep Time
10 Minutes

 Cooking Time
25 Minutes

INGREDIENTS

1 lb. brussel sprouts

1 tablespoon sesame oil

1 teaspoon salt

1 teaspoon white pepper

1 teaspoon garlic powder

1 tablespoon teriyaki sauce

1 tablespoon sugar

1 tablespoon sesame seeds

DIRECTIONS 4

TO PREPARE THESE TASTY BRUSSELS SPROUTS, START BY HALVING THEM. TRANSFER THE HALVES INTO A SPACIOUS BOWL. NEXT, INCORPORATE SESAME OIL, SALT, PEPPER, GARLIC POWDER, TERIYAKI SAUCE, AND SUGAR, THEN MIX THOROUGHLY. ARRANGE THE SPROUTS ON A BAKING SHEET LINED WITH PARCHMENT PAPER. BAKE IN A PREHEATED 375°F OVEN FOR APPROXIMATELY 25 MINUTES, OR UNTIL THEY BECOME TENDER. ONCE OUT OF THE OVEN, PROMPTLY SPRINKLE WITH TOASTED SESAME SEEDS. NOW, SAVOR THE DELICIOUSNESS!

YELLOW RICE

 Prep Time
10 Minutes

 Cooking Time
25 Minutes

INGREDIENTS

2 cups jasmine rice

3 cups chicken broth

½ red pepper
(finely chopped)

½ yellow pepper
(finely chopped)

½ orange pepper
(finely chopped)

½ medium onion
(finely chopped)

2 tablespoons avocado

2 tablespoons butter

3 garlic cloves (finely
chopped)

1 teaspoon onion
powder

1 teaspoon garlic
powder

1 teaspoon creole
seasoning

1 teaspoon thyme

1 teaspoon parsley

Salt to taste

1 teaspoon turmeric

3 cups chicken broth

1 chicken bouillon
packet

DIRECTIONS 6

TO CREATE THIS DELIGHTFUL YELLOW RICE, BEGIN BY RINSING THE RICE UNTIL THE WATER RUNS CLEAR, THEN SET IT ASIDE. IN A LARGE POT, HEAT SOME OIL AND ADD BUTTER, FOLLOWED BY THE PEPPERS AND ONIONS. SAUTÉ UNTIL THEY BECOME TENDER, THEN INCORPORATE THE GARLIC. COOK FOR AN ADDITIONAL MINUTE BEFORE ADDING THE RICE, MIXING WELL. ALLOW IT TO COOK FOR ABOUT FOUR MINUTES, THEN STIR IN THE GARLIC POWDER, ONION POWDER, CREOLE SEASONING, THYME, PARSLEY, SALT, PEPPER, AND TURMERIC. NEXT, POUR IN THE CHICKEN BROTH ALONG WITH THE CHICKEN BOUILLON PACKET, STIRRING ONCE MORE. BRING THE MIXTURE TO A BOIL, THEN COVER, REDUCE THE HEAT, AND LET IT SIMMER FOR APPROXIMATELY 20 MINUTES. ONCE DONE, REMOVE THE LID, FLUFF THE RICE WITH A FORK, AND SAVOR YOUR MEAL!

KELLZ REFLECTION

As a young girl, I vividly remembers the magical sight of our kitchen table overflowing with an array of sweets, cakes, and pies. The table was a colorful tapestry of deliciousness, each dessert more beautiful than the last. The cakes were adorned with intricate frosting designs, the pies had perfectly golden crusts, and the sweets sparkled with a sugary sheen. I was in awe of how stunning everything looked, almost too perfect to eat. The kitchen, usually a place of bustling activity, now felt like a wonderland of treats, each one a testament to my mother's incredible baking skills.

The joy she felt in those moments was immeasurable. Seeing all the hard work my mom had put into creating such a feast filled her with pride and happiness. I loved watching my mom bake, but seeing the final result laid out so perfectly was something else entirely. It was a celebration of love and effort, and I felt a deep sense of gratitude for those sweet moments. The kitchen table, laden with desserts, wasn't just a sight to behold; it was a symbol of my mother's dedication and the joy of sharing those delightful creations with family and friends.

DESSERTS

Open with ▾

BANANA PUDDING

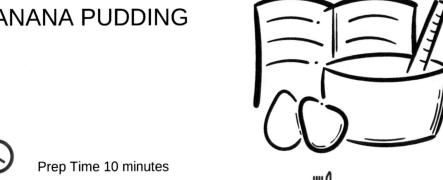

 Prep Time 10 minutes

Cooking Time
30 Minutes

INGREDIENTS

6 bananas

1 tablespoon lemon juice

3 cups milk

2 ¼ cups sugar

½ cup all-purpose flour

½ teaspoon salt

4 large eggs(separated)

2 -11oz boxes of Nilla Wafers

 9x 13 inch

6

DIRECTIONS

TO PREPARE SOUTHERN BANANA PUDDING, START BY COMBINING 3 CUPS OF MILK, 2 CUPS OF SUGAR, ½ CUP OF FLOUR, AND ½ TEASPOON OF SALT IN A MEDIUM POT. HEAT THE MIXTURE OVER MEDIUM HEAT,STIRRING CONSTANTLY WITH A WHISK UNTIL THICKENED. TEMPER THE EGG YOLKS BY GRADUALLY ADDING A SPOONFUL OF THE HOT PUDDING MIXTURE, STIRRING RAPIDLY TO PREVENT SCRAMBLING. THEN, POUR THE EGG YOLKS INTO THE PUDDING, STIRRING CONTINUOUSLY TO PREVENT CLUMPING. COOK FOR AN ADDITIONAL 3 MINUTES, STIRRING CONSTANTLY, UNTIL THICKENED. REMOVE FROM HEAT AND INCORPORATE VANILLA EXTRACT. MEANWHILE, PEEL AND SLICE BANANAS, PLACING THEM IN A BOWL WITH FRESH LEMON JUICE. IN A 9X13-INCH BAKING DISH, CREATE LAYERS OF NILLA WAFERS, BANANAS, AND PUDDING,REPEATING UNTIL THE TOP IS REACHED. SET ASIDE TO PREPARE THE MERINGUE. IN A MEDIUM BOWL, WHIP 4 EGG WHITES AND ¼ CUP OF SUGAR UNTIL STIFF PEAKS FORM. SPREAD EVENLY OVER THE PUDDING AND BAKE IN A 375-DEGREE OVEN FOR 12 MINUTES, OR UNTIL GOLDEN BROWN.ALLOW TO COOL BEFORE SERVING, EITHER WARM OR CHILLED.

BLUEBERRY COBBLER

 Prep Time 15 minutes

 Cooking Time
1 hour

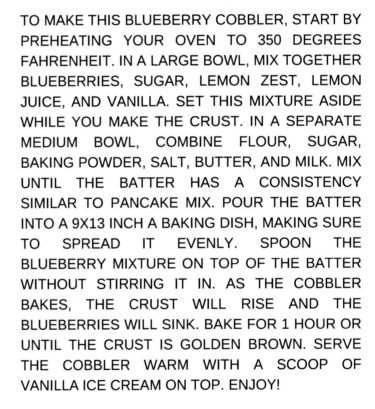 6

INGREDIENTS

DIRECTIONS

32oz Fresh Blueberries

1 ½ cup sugar

2 tablespoons lemon juice

1 tablespoon lemon zest

1 teaspoon vanilla

The Crust

2 cups all purpose flour

1 cup sugar

12 tablespoons baking powder

½ teaspoon salt

¾ cup butter

1 to 1 ½ cups milk

TO MAKE THIS BLUEBERRY COBBLER, START BY PREHEATING YOUR OVEN TO 350 DEGREES FAHRENHEIT. IN A LARGE BOWL, MIX TOGETHER BLUEBERRIES, SUGAR, LEMON ZEST, LEMON JUICE, AND VANILLA. SET THIS MIXTURE ASIDE WHILE YOU MAKE THE CRUST. IN A SEPARATE MEDIUM BOWL, COMBINE FLOUR, SUGAR, BAKING POWDER, SALT, BUTTER, AND MILK. MIX UNTIL THE BATTER HAS A CONSISTENCY SIMILAR TO PANCAKE MIX. POUR THE BATTER INTO A 9X13 INCH A BAKING DISH, MAKING SURE TO SPREAD IT EVENLY. SPOON THE BLUEBERRY MIXTURE ON TOP OF THE BATTER WITHOUT STIRRING IT IN. AS THE COBBLER BAKES, THE CRUST WILL RISE AND THE BLUEBERRIES WILL SINK. BAKE FOR 1 HOUR OR UNTIL THE CRUST IS GOLDEN BROWN. SERVE THE COBBLER WARM WITH A SCOOP OF VANILLA ICE CREAM ON TOP. ENJOY!

BREAD PUDDING

Prep Time
20 minutes

Cooking Time
45 Minutes

INGREDIENTS

8 slices day-old brioche
bread, Cut into small
pieces
2 tablespoons unsalted
melted butter
½ cup raisins (red or
black) (Optional)
½ cup golden raisins
(Optional)
2 cups milk
½ cup white sugar
½ cup brown sugar
2 tablespoons unsalted
butter, melted

4 large eggs, beaten
1 teaspoon vanilla
extract
1 teaspoon ground
cinnamon
½ teaspoon nutmeg
THE SAUCE
2 tablespoons butter
½ cup brown sugar
1 cup milk
1 tablespoons Rum
extract or ¼ cup dark
rum
THE SLURRY
 1 tablespoon
cornstarch
1 1/2 tablespoon water

DIRECTIONS 6

TO CREATE THIS DELECTABLE BREAD PUDDING, START BY
REHYDRATING THE RAISINS. PLACE THE RAISINS IN A BOWL
OF WATER FOR ABOUT 10 MINUTES OR UNTIL THEY SOFTEN.
ONCE DONE, DRAIN THE WATER AND SET THE RAISINS
ASIDE. NEXT, SLICE THE BRIOCHE BREAD INTO BITE-SIZED
PIECES AND ADD THEM TO ANOTHER BOWL, SETTING IT
ASIDE AS WELL. IN A SEPARATE BOWL, COMBINE MILK,
WHITE SUGAR, BROWN SUGAR, BUTTER, EGGS, VANILLA,
CINNAMON, AND NUTMEG, MIXING EVERYTHING TOGETHER
THOROUGHLY.

BEGIN LAYERING BY PLACING SOME BREAD CHUNKS IN A
BAKING DISH, FOLLOWED BY A LAYER OF RAISINS. REPEAT
THIS PROCESS UNTIL ALL THE BREAD AND RAISINS ARE
LAYERED. POUR THE MILK AND EGG MIXTURE OVER THE
LAYERED BREAD AND RAISINS, THEN USE A SPATULA TO
GENTLY PRESS THE BREAD DOWN, ENSURING IT ABSORBS
THE MIXTURE. BAKE IN A PREHEATED OVEN AT 350 DEGREES
FOR 45 MINUTES, OR UNTIL A TOOTHPICK INSERTED COMES
OUT CLEAN AND THE TOP IS GOLDEN BROWN. ONCE
FINISHED, REMOVE FROM THE OVEN AND LET IT REST.

WHILE THE PUDDING IS RESTING, PREPARE THE GLAZE. IN A
MEDIUM POT, COMBINE BUTTER AND BROWN SUGAR, MIXING
UNTIL INCORPORATED. THEN, ADD IN THE MILK AND RUM.
BRING THE MIXTURE TO A BOIL, AND ONCE BOILING, ADD IN
THE SLURRY, WHICH IS A MIX OF CORNSTARCH AND WATER.
WHEN THE GLAZE THICKENS, POUR IT OVER THE WARM
BREAD PUDDING. ENJOY YOUR DELICIOUS CREATION WHILE
IT'S WARM!

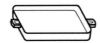 9x13 Inch

CINNAMON ROLLS

 Prep Time 2 Hours

 Cooking Time 25 Minutes

INGREDIENTS

1 1/4 cup lukewarm whole milk

4 teaspoons yeast

4 cups bread flour

1/2 cup sugar

1 teaspoon salt

2 large eggs (beaten)

The Filling

4 tablespoons butter

1/2 cup white sugar

1/2 cup brown sugar

1/4 cup cinnamon

The Glaze

2 cups confectioners' sugar

1 teaspoon butter

1 to 3 tablespoons milk

½ teaspoon vanilla

DIRECTIONS 6

TO PREPARE THESE DELICIOUS CINNAMON ROLLS, FOLLOW THESE STEPS: POUR ROOM TEMPERATURE MILK INTO A BOWL AND ADD THE ACTIVE DRY YEAST. ALLOW IT TO SIT FOR ABOUT 5 MINUTES FOR THE YEAST TO ACTIVATE. WHILE THE YEAST IS ACTIVATING, MIX BREAD FLOUR, SUGAR, AND SALT USING THE WHISK ATTACHMENT ON YOUR MIXER UNTIL WELL COMBINED. ONCE THE YEAST IS ACTIVATED, SWITCH TO THE DOUGH HOOK ATTACHMENT, AND ADD IT TO THE FLOUR MIXTURE. INCORPORATE THE EGGS AND BUTTER AND CONTINUE MIXING UNTIL THE DOUGH CLINGS TO THE MIXER. LET THE DOUGH REST FOR A MINUTE, THEN TRANSFER IT TO A FLOURED SURFACE. KNEAD THE DOUGH FOR SIX MINUTES. PLACE THE DOUGH IN A LARGE, GREASED BOWL, COVER IT WITH PLASTIC WRAP, AND LET IT RISE IN A WARM PLACE (I USE MY STOVE TOP) FOR ABOUT AN HOUR AND A HALF UNTIL IT DOUBLES IN SIZE. ONCE THE DOUGH HAS DOUBLED, DEFLATE IT BY PUNCHING THE CENTER, THEN ROLL IT OUT ON A FLOURED SURFACE TO ABOUT 1/4-INCH THICKNESS WITH A ROLLING PIN. SPREAD SOFTENED BUTTER OVER THE DOUGH, SPRINKLE BROWN SUGAR, WHITE SUGAR, AND CINNAMON ON, THEN ROLL IT INTO A LOG. CUT THE LOG IN HALF, THEN SLICE IT INTO INDIVIDUAL CINNAMON ROLLS AND PLACE THEM ON A GREASED BAKING SHEET. COVER THE ROLLS WITH A CLEAN TOWEL AND LET THEM RISE IN A WARM SPOT FOR ANOTHER 45 MINUTES UNTIL DOUBLED IN SIZE. BAKE THE ROLLS AT 350 DEGREES FOR ABOUT 25 MINUTES UNTIL THEY REACH YOUR DESIRED BROWNNESS. WHILE THE ROLLS BAKE, PREPARE THE GLAZE BY MIXING CONFECTIONER'S SUGAR, BUTTER, VANILLA, AND SWEET CREAM UNTIL SMOOTH. ONCE THE CINNAMON ROLLS ARE DONE, DRIZZLE THEM WITH THE GLAZE, SERVE WARM, AND ENJOY!

102

PEACH COBBLER

 Prep Time
20 Minutes

 Cooking Time
1 Hour

INGREDIENTS

8 large peaches (peeled and cut)

½ cup white sugar

½ cup brown sugar

1 tablespoon cinnamon

¼ teaspoon nutmeg

1 teaspoon vanilla

1 tablespoon cornstarch

¼ cup butter

The Crust

1 ½ cup all-purpose flour

½ cup sugar

1 tablespoon baking powder

1/4 teaspoon salt

½ cup melted butter

1 to 1 ½ cups milk

DIRECTIONS 6

TO PREPARE THIS DELICIOUS PEACH COBBLER, FOLLOW THESE STEPS: A LARGE POT, COMBINE PEACHES, WHITE SUGAR, BROWN SUGAR, CINNAMON, NUTMEG, VANILLA, CORNSTARCH, AND BUTTER. COOK ON MEDIUM HEAT FOR A FEW MINUTES UNTIL THE SUGAR DISSOLVES AND THE PEACHES RELEASE THEIR JUICES. CONTINUE COOKING UNTIL THE PEACHES ARE TENDER AND A THICK SYRUP FORMS, THEN SET ASIDE. FOR THE CRUST, MIX FLOUR, BAKING POWDER, SALT, BUTTER, AND MILK IN A LARGE BOWL UNTIL WELL COMBINED. SPREAD THE CRUST EVENLY IN A 9X13 INCH BAKING DISH, THEN SPOON THE PEACHES ON TOP WITHOUT STIRRING TO PREVENT THE CRUST FROM COVERING THEM. BAKE AT 350 DEGREES FOR AN HOUR OR UNTIL A TOOTHPICK COMES OUT CLEAN AND THE COBBLER IS GOLDEN BROWN. LET IT COOL SLIGHTLY OR ENJOY IT HOT, AND DON'T FORGET TO SERVE IT WITH A SCOOP OF VANILLA BEAN ICE CREAM FOR A DELIGHTFUL TREAT.

9x13 inch

★★★★☆

RICE PUDDING

Prep Time
15 minutes

Cooking Time
55 Minutes

INGREDIENTS

3 cups day old rice

1 ½ cup sugar

½ stick butter

3 eggs

1 cup milk

1 cup cream

½ teaspoon cinnamon

½ teaspoon nutmeg.

DIRECTIONS 6

TO PREPARE RICE PUDDING, GATHER A LARGE BOWL AND A 9X13 INCH BAKING DISH. BEGIN BY BLENDING BUTTER AND SUGAR IN THE BOWL UNTIL SMOOTH. THEN, MIX IN EGGS, MILK, AND CREAM THOROUGHLY. ADD RICE, CINNAMON, AND NUTMEG, AND GIVE IT A QUICK STIR. TRANSFER THE MIXTURE INTO THE BUTTERED BAKING DISH AND BAKE AT 365 DEGREES FOR 45 TO 55 MINUTES. ONCE COOKED, ALLOW IT TO COOL BEFORE SERVING. INDULGE IN THE DELIGHTFUL AND COMFORTING RICE PUDDING!

DRINKS

LEMONADE

 Prep Time
10 Minutes

 Cooking Time
5 Minutes

INGREDIENTS

2 cups fresh lemon juice

2 cups of sugar

2 cups of water

-Extras-

Fresh Mints

Lemon Slices

DIRECTIONS 8

TO CREATE THIS REFRESHING LEMONADE, START BY COMBINING SUGAR AND WATER IN A MEDIUM POT AND BRING IT TO A BOIL. ONCE THE MIXTURE TRANSFORMS INTO A SYRUP, REMOVE IT FROM THE HEAT AND POUR IT INTO A LARGE PITCHER. NEXT, ADD THE LEMON JUICE AND FILL THE REMAINDER OF THE PITCHER WITH WATER. STIR WELL TO BLEND THE INGREDIENTS, THEN POUR IT OVER A GLASS FILLED WITH ICE AND SAVOR! FOR AN EXTRA TOUCH OF FRESHNESS, MIX IN A BIT OF MINT AND SOME LEMON SLICES. ENJOY!

PINEAPPLE LEMONADE

 Prep Time
10 Minutes

DIRECTIONS 8

INGREDIENTS

2 cups country time lemonade

1 quart pineapple juice

1 cup sugar

water

IN A LARGE PITCHER, COMBINE COUNTRY TIME LEMONADE, PINEAPPLE JUICE, SUGAR, AND WATER. MIX THOROUGHLY UNTIL WELL BLENDED. POUR INTO A GLASS FILLED WITH ICE AND ENJOY!

SOUTHERN SWEET TEA

 Prep Time
5 Minutes

 Cooking Time
20 MINUTES

INGREDIENTS

16 cups water

3 large family size tea bags

2 cups sugar

DIRECTIONS 8

TO PREPARE THIS DELIGHTFUL SWEET TEA, FOLLOW THESE STEPS. IN A MEDIUM POT, COMBINE 2 CUPS OF WATER WITH 3 LARGE TEA BAGS AND HEAT IT OVER MEDIUM HEAT. ONCE IT REACHES A BOIL, COVER THE POT WITH A LID, TURN OFF THE HEAT, AND ALLOW IT TO STEEP FOR 20 MINUTES. AFTER STEEPING, REMOVE THE TEA BAGS AND POUR THE TEA INTO A GALLON JUG. FILL THE JUG WITH WATER AND THEN ADD THE SUGAR. STIR UNTIL ALL THE SUGAR IS COMPLETELY DISSOLVED. SERVE OVER ICE AND ENJOY!

YOU, ME AND A CUP OF TEA

HOLIDAY BONUS

CANDIED YAMS

 Prep Time
10 minutes

 Cooking Time
25 to 30 Minutes

INGREDIENTS

3 large sweet potatoes

2 cups water

1/2 stick butter

1/2 cup white sugar

1/2 cup brown sugar

1 tablespoons cinnamon

1 teaspoons nutmeg

DIRECTIONS 4

BEGIN BY PEELING AND CUTTING THE POTATOES INTO 1-INCH PIECES, THEN HALVE THOSE PIECES. RINSE THEM THOROUGHLY BEFORE PLACING THEM IN A POT. COVER THE POTATOES WITH WATER AND SET THE POT ON THE STOVE OVER MEDIUM HEAT. COOK UNTIL THEY ARE FORK-TENDER, WHICH SHOULD TAKE AROUND 12 MINUTES. ONCE COOKED, DRAIN THE WATER AND ADD IN THE BUTTER, WHITE SUGAR, BROWN SUGAR, CINNAMON, AND NUTMEG. RETURN THE POT TO THE STOVE AND COOK FOR AN ADDITIONAL 10 MINUTES, ALLOWING THE SUGARS TO MELT AND CREATE A SYRUP. ALLOW TO COOL, AND THEN ENJOY YOUR DELICIOUS DISH!

CHICKEN & STOCK

 Prep Time 15 minutes

 Cooking Time
2 hours

INGREDIENTS

1 whole chicken

6 cups of water

3 stalks celery chopped

3 stalks carrots chopped

3 garlic cloves chopped

1 tablespoon creole
seasoning

1 tablespoon garlic powder

1 tablespoon onion powder

1 tablespoon caramelized
onion butter (I use Kinder's)

1 tablespoon 24 herbs and
spices

★★★★☆

 4

DIRECTIONS

COMBINE ALL THE INGREDIENTS IN A LARGE POT AND COOK OVER MEDIUM HEAT FOR APPROXIMATELY TWO HOURS, OR UNTIL THE CHICKEN IS TENDER. ONCE DONE, TAKE THE CHICKEN OUT OF THE POT AND STRAIN THE STOCK INTO A JAR. THIS STOCK CAN BE USED IN ANY RECIPE THAT REQUIRES CHICKEN STOCK.

COLLARD GREENS

 Prep Time
30 Minutes

 Cooking Time
3 Hours

INGREDIENTS

3 bunches of fresh
collard greens
1 pack of smoked
turkey wings
(should be about 2
wings)
2 tablespoons olive oil
1 whole onion chopped
1 fresh garlic cloves
chopped
4 cups chicken stock
1 cup water

1 serrano pepper
chopped
1 tablespoon garlic
powder
1 tablespoon onion
powder
salt and pepper to taste
The Cleaning
1 teaspoon baking soda
1 tablespoon apple
cider vinegar
Full bowl of Water

DIRECTIONS 6

TO PREPARE THESE TASTY COLLARD GREENS, BEGIN BY THOROUGHLY CLEANING THEM THROUGH A TRIPLE WASH. I PREFER USING APPLE CIDER VINEGAR AND BAKING SODA FOR THIS PROCESS. FILL TWO BOWLS WITH WATER, ALONG WITH BAKING SODA AND VINEGAR, AND WASH THE COLLARD GREENS THREE TO FOUR TIMES UNTIL NO GRIT OR SAND REMAINS. REMEMBER TO REFRESH THE BOWLS WITH FRESH WATER, VINEGAR, AND BAKING SODA EACH TIME. ONCE THE GREENS ARE CLEAN, THEY ARE READY TO COOK.

IN A LARGE POT, PREHEAT OIL OVER MEDIUM HEAT AND ADD THE ONIONS. SAUTÉ THE ONIONS UNTIL THEY BECOME TRANSLUCENT, WHICH SHOULD TAKE ABOUT TWO TO THREE MINUTES, AND THEN INCORPORATE THE GARLIC. COOK THE GARLIC FOR AN ADDITIONAL MINUTE BEFORE ADDING THE COLLARD GREENS. POUR IN THE CHICKEN STOCK AND WATER, ENSURING NOT TO OVERFILL THE POT TO PREVENT BOILING OVER WHEN HEATED.

PLACE THE SMOKED TURKEY ON TOP OF THE GREENS AND COVER THE POT WITH A LID. LET IT COOK FOR ONE HOUR, THEN INTRODUCE THE CHOPPED SERRANO PEPPERS, GARLIC POWDER, AND ONION POWDER, MIXING EVERYTHING WELL BEFORE PLACING THE LID BACK ON. CHECK THE POT EVERY HOUR TO ENSURE THAT THE SMOKED TURKEY BECOMES TENDER AND FALLS OFF THE BONE—THIS SHOULD OCCUR AFTER APPROXIMATELY THREE HOURS. ONCE THE MEAT HAS FALLEN OFF THE BONE, REMOVE THE BONES FROM THE COLLARD GREENS AND DISCARD THEM.

YOUR GREENS ARE NOW READY! JUST ADD SOME SALT AND PEPPER, AND DON'T FORGET TO SERVE WITH CORNBREAD. ENJOY!

CRANBERRY SAUCE

 Prep Time 10 minutes

 Cooking Time
15 Minutes

4

INGREDIENTS

2 12oz packs of

cranberries

1 1/2 cup sugar

2 tablespoon orange zest

1/2 cup orange juice

1 cup water

1 cinnamon stick

1/4 teaspoon nutmeg

1/2 teaspoon salt

1 teaspoon vanilla

 ★★★★☆

DIRECTIONS

TO PREPARE THIS DELIGHTFUL CRANBERRY SAUCE, START BY PLACING CRANBERRIES IN A LARGE POT OVER MEDIUM HEAT. NEXT, MIX IN SUGAR, ORANGE ZEST, ORANGE JUICE, WATER, CINNAMON, NUTMEG, SALT, AND VANILLA. STIR OCCASIONALLY AND LET THE CRANBERRIES COOK UNTIL THEY BURST, WHICH TAKES APPROXIMATELY 7 TO 8 MINUTES. ONCE DONE, REMOVE THE CINNAMON STICK.

AT THIS STAGE, YOU CAN EITHER TRANSFER THE WHOLE CRANBERRIES INTO CONTAINERS FOR A CHUNKY SAUCE OR BLEND THEM FOR A GEL-LIKE CONSISTENCY. FOR JELLED CRANBERRY SAUCE, USE AN IMMERSION BLENDER TO PUREE THE CRANBERRIES UNTIL SMOOTH. THEN, INCORPORATE A CORNSTARCH SLURRY AND COOK FOR AN ADDITIONAL 1 TO 2 MINUTES BEFORE REMOVING FROM HEAT.

IMMEDIATELY POUR THE MIXTURE INTO CONTAINERS AND ALLOW IT TO SET. REFRIGERATE OVERNIGHT AND SERVE CHILLED.

KELLZ REFLECTION

I fondly remembers Thanksgiving Day, sitting at the table with my mother and grandmother, surrounded by the mouthwatering aroma of turkey, stuffing, and freshly baked pies. The kitchen was a symphony of delicious scents that made my heart swell with anticipation. As we sat down to eat, I felt an overwhelming sense of love and warmth. The table was beautifully set, and the food looked like a feast fit for royalty. Every bite was a taste of home, filled with the flavors of tradition and the love my family poured into each dish.

Listening to my mothers old stories was one of my favorite parts of the day. The tales of past Thanksgivings, family adventures, and cherished memories brought laughter and joy to everyone around the table. The sound of my family's laughter was like music, filling the room with happiness. I felt so grateful to God for these moments, for the love of my family, and for the blessings we shared. Thanksgiving was more than just a meal; it was a celebration of togetherness, love, and gratitude, and I cherished every second of it.

GIBLET GRAVY

 Prep Time
15 Minutes

 Cooking Time
2 1/2 Hours

INGREDIENTS

Turkey Neck and
Giblets from a
whole turkey
4 cups water
2 tablespoons olive oil
1 cup chopped celery
1 cup onion chopped
2 garlic cloves chopped
1 sprig rosemary
1 sprig thyme
1 sprig parsley

1 tablespoon chicken
bouillon
1 teaspoon poultry
seasoning
1 teaspoon garlic
powder
1 teaspoon creole
(optional)
1 teaspoon sage
1 boiled egg chopped
1 cup heavy cream
corn starch slurry
1 teaspoon pepper

DIRECTIONS 6

TO CREATE THIS DELIGHTFUL GIBLET GRAVY, BEGIN BY PLACING A MEDIUM POT ON THE STOVE OVER MEDIUM HEAT. POUR IN THE OLIVE OIL, AND ONCE IT'S HEATED, ADD THE TURKEY NECK AND GIBLETS. SEAR THEM ON ALL SIDES TO ENHANCE THE FLAVOR, THEN INCORPORATE THE ONIONS AND CELERY. COOK UNTIL THEY BECOME TENDER, THEN ADD THE GARLIC AND SAUTÉ UNTIL FRAGRANT, ROUGHLY ONE MINUTE. NEXT, STIR IN THE WATER, ROSEMARY, THYME, PARSLEY, CHICKEN BOUILLON, POULTRY SEASONING, GARLIC POWDER, CREOLE SEASONING, AND SAGE. LOWER THE HEAT TO A SIMMER AND ALLOW IT TO COOK UNTIL THE MEAT IS TENDER, WHICH SHOULD TAKE ABOUT 1½ TO 2 HOURS. AFTERWARD, REMOVE THE MEAT AND STRAIN THE BROTH. SHRED THE MEAT FROM THE TURKEY NECK AND CHOP THE GIBLETS. RETURN THE BROTH TO THE POT, THEN MIX IN THE GIBLETS AND THE MEAT FROM THE TURKEY NECK. ADD THE EGG AND BRING THE MIXTURE BACK TO A BOIL. STIR IN THE HEAVY CREAM AND THE CORNSTARCH SLURRY (A BLEND OF CORNSTARCH AND WATER) AND LET IT THICKEN INTO A GRAVY. FINALLY, ADD THE BLACK PEPPER AND LET IT SIMMER FOR ABOUT 15 MINUTES. POUR IT OVER YOUR TURKEY AND DRESSING AND ENJOY!

119

KEYLIME CAKE

 Prep Time
15 Minutes

 Cooking Time
25 TO 30 MINUTES

INGREDIENTS

1 packs lemon cake mix

1 3oz packs lime Gelatin

4 eggs at room temp

1/3 cup key lime juice

1/2 cup vegetable oil

1/2 cup water

1 teaspoon vanilla

2 8' round cake pan

Frosting

1 8oz pack cream cheese

1/2 cup softened butter

4 cups confectioners' sugar

2 tablespoons international

delight, sweet cream

1 teaspoon vanilla

DIRECTIONS 6

TO CREATE THIS DELECTABLE CAKE, BEGIN BY PREPARING THE CAKE PANS. SPRAY THEM WITH NONSTICK FLOUR COOKING SPRAY AND SET ASIDE. IN A STAND MIXER, COMBINE THE CAKE MIX AND GELATIN MIX. NEXT, INCORPORATE THE EGGS, LIME JUICE, VEGETABLE OIL, WATER, AND VANILLA, MIXING EVERYTHING THOROUGHLY. POUR THE BATTER INTO THE PREPARED PANS AND BAKE IN A PREHEATED OVEN AT 350 DEGREES FOR 20 TO 25 MINUTES. ONCE DONE, REMOVE THEM FROM THE OVEN AND LET THEM COOL COMPLETELY ON A COOLING RACK. NOW, IT'S TIME TO MAKE THE FROSTING. IN THE STAND MIXER, BLEND THE CREAM CHEESE AND BUTTER UNTIL WELL COMBINED. THEN, ADD THE CONFECTIONERS' SUGAR, SWEET CREAM, AND VANILLA, MIXING UNTIL THE FROSTING IS SMOOTH. IF THE MIXTURE FEELS TOO DRY, SIMPLY ADD MORE SWEET CREAM. ONCE THE CAKE HAS COOLED, SPREAD THE ICING ON TOP AND ENJOY!

LEMON POUND CAKE

 Prep Time
20 Minutes

 Cooking Time
1 Hour 10 MINUTES

INGREDIENTS

Bakers Baking Spray (for the pan)

1 ½ cups unsalted butter

3 cups sugar

5 large eggs

¼ cup lemon juice

1 tablespoon vanilla

3 cups all-purpose flour

½ teaspoon baking powder

½ teaspoon salt

1 cup milk

¼ cup sour cream

THE GLAZE

3 tablespoons lemon juice

3 to 4 cups confectioners' sugar

(glaze should be smooth)

1 tablespoon milk

½ teaspoon vanilla

DIRECTIONS 8

TO MAKE THIS TASTY POUND CAKE: START BY SPRAYING THE PANS WITH BAKER'S SPRAY AND SETTING THEM ASIDE. SIFT THE FLOUR INTO A BOWL, AND THEN MIX IN THE BAKING POWDER AND SALT. IN A MIXER, COMBINE THE BUTTER AND SUGAR, BEATING THEM FOR 8 MINUTES UNTIL THEY BECOME FLUFFY. CRACK THE EGGS INTO A SEPARATE BOWL TO CHECK FOR ANY IMPERFECTIONS, THEN ADD THEM TO THE MIXTURE ONE AT A TIME. BE SURE TO SCRAPE DOWN THE SIDES OF THE BOWL FOR EVEN MIXING. BLEND IN THE LEMON JUICE AND VANILLA EXTRACT. GRADUALLY ALTERNATE ADDING THE FLOUR AND MILK, BEGINNING AND ENDING WITH THE FLOUR. FINALLY, MIX IN THE SOUR CREAM. USE A SPATULA TO STIR EVERYTHING WELL FOR A THOROUGH BLEND, THEN POUR THE BATTER INTO THE PREPARED PANS. BAKE IN THE OVEN FOR 45 MINUTES, THEN CHECK FOR RISING AND BROWNING. IF NECESSARY, EXTEND THE BAKING TIME BY ANOTHER 15 TO 20 MINUTES. TO TEST FOR DONENESS, INSERT A TOOTHPICK INTO THE CENTER; IF IT COMES OUT CLEAN, THE CAKE IS READY. IF NOT, RETURN IT TO THE OVEN, CHECKING EVERY 10 MINUTES UNTIL IT IS FULLY BAKED. THE TOTAL COOKING TIME SHOULD NOT EXCEED 1 HOUR AND 10 MINUTES, SO PATIENCE IS ESSENTIAL. ONCE DONE, REMOVE FROM THE OVEN AND LET COOL FOR ABOUT 10 MINUTES BEFORE APPLYING THE GLAZE. TO MAKE THE GLAZE, COMBINE LEMON JUICE, CONFECTIONERS' SUGAR, MILK, AND VANILLA IN A MEDIUM BOWL. MIX UNTIL INCORPORATED, THEN POUR OVER THE CAKE WHILE IT IS STILL WARM. NOW, ENJOY!

PINEAPPLE GLAZED HAM

 Prep Time 20 minutes

 Cooking Time
3 hour 25 Minutes

INGREDIENTS

10lb. ham

1 ½ pineapple Juice

1 cup white sugar

1 cup brown sugar

1 corn starch slurry

Cornstarch Slurry

1 tablespoon cornstarch

1 ½ tablespoons water

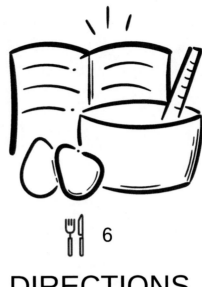

6

DIRECTIONS

TO PREPARE THIS MOUTHWATERING HAM, START BY COMBINING PINEAPPLE JUICE, WHITE SUGAR, AND BROWN SUGAR IN A MEDIUM POT. MIX WELL AND PLACE IT ON THE STOVE OVER MEDIUM HEAT. COOK UNTIL THE SUGARS COMPLETELY DISSOLVE. AFTER THE SUGARS HAVE MELTED, ALLOW IT TO COOK FOR AN ADDITIONAL THREE MINUTES, BEING CAREFUL NOT TO LET IT BOIL OVER. NEXT, ADD YOUR CORNSTARCH SLURRY AND STIR CONTINUOUSLY UNTIL THE MIXTURE THICKENS. REMOVE IT FROM THE HEAT AND LET IT COOL. PLACE THE HAM IN A FOIL-LINED PAN AND GENEROUSLY SPREAD THE GLAZE OVER IT, THEN COVER WITH FOIL. THE FOIL WILL KEEP THE SUGARS FROM BURNING ON THE HAM. BAKE IN A PREHEATED OVEN AT 375°F FOR ONE HOUR. AFTER THAT, IT'S TIME TO BASTE THE HAM. CAREFULLY TAKE IT OUT OF THE OVEN, USE A SPOON TO GATHER THE JUICES AT THE BOTTOM, AND POUR THEM OVER THE HAM. REPEAT THIS PROCESS ABOUT FIVE OR SIX TIMES, THEN RETURN THE HAM TO THE OVEN FOR ANOTHER HOUR. AFTER THE SECOND HOUR, TAKE THE HAM OUT AGAIN AND BASTE IT THOROUGHLY BEFORE COVERING IT ONCE MORE AND PUTTING IT BACK IN THE OVEN FOR ANOTHER HOUR. CONTINUE TO BASTE THE HAM EVERY HOUR ACCORDING TO ITS WEIGHT AND COOKING TIME. FOR THIS 10-POUND HAM, IT WILL COOK FOR A TOTAL OF THREE HOURS, SO REMEMBER TO BASTE IT HOURLY UNTIL THE COOKING TIME IS COMPLETE. ONCE THE THREE HOURS ARE UP AND THE INTERNAL TEMPERATURE REACHES 145°F, REMOVE IT FROM THE OVEN. SPREAD THE REMAINING GLAZE ON TOP AND RETURN IT TO THE OVEN UNCOVERED FOR ABOUT 20 MINUTES TO ALLOW THE GLAZE TO SET. FINALLY, POUR A LITTLE MORE OF THE JUICES FROM THE PAN OVER THE HAM, LET IT REST FOR 20 MINUTES, AND ENJOY YOUR DELICIOUS CREATION!

SMOTHERED TURKEY WINGS

Prep Time
20 minutes

Cooking Time
2 Hours 30 Minutes

INGREDIENTS

8 whole turkey wings

1/3 cup olive oil

2 tablespoons Creole seasoning

2 tablespoons Onion Powder

2 tablespoons Garlic powder

2 tablespoons Kinder's Poultry Butter Blend

2 tablespoons Kinder's caramelized onion butter

2 tablespoons Bragg 24 herbs and spices

14 oz can chicken broth

The Gravy

3 cans chicken broth

1 pack chicken bouillon

Cornstarch slurry

Cornstarch Slurry

2 tablespoons cornstarch

3 tablespoons water

DIRECTIONS 8

TO CREATE THESE DELECTABLE TURKEY WINGS, START BY ARRANGING THE WINGS IN A LARGE ROASTING PAN. SEASON THEM GENEROUSLY WITH CREOLE SEASONING, ONION POWDER, GARLIC POWDER, KINDER'S POULTRY BUTTER BLEND, KINDER'S CARAMELIZED ONION BUTTER, AND BRAGG'S 24 HERBS AND SPICES TO BUILD A FLAVORFUL BASE. POUR IN CHICKEN BROTH, COVER THE PAN, AND BAKE IN A PREHEATED OVEN AT 375 DEGREES FOR ONE HOUR. AFTER THIS TIME, TAKE THEM OUT AND FLIP THE TURKEY WINGS FOR EVEN COOKING. COVER THEM AGAIN AND RETURN TO THE OVEN FOR ANOTHER HOUR. ONCE THE HOUR IS UP, REMOVE THE TURKEY WINGS FROM THE OVEN AND UNCOVER THEM. BAKE UNCOVERED FOR AN ADDITIONAL 15 MINUTES TO ACHIEVE PERFECT BROWNING. WHILE THE WINGS ARE BROWNING, PREPARE THE GRAVY BY COMBINING 3 CUPS OF CHICKEN BROTH WITH A CHICKEN BOUILLON PACKET AND A CORNSTARCH SLURRY (MADE FROM CORNSTARCH AND WATER) COOK ON MEDIUM HEAT UNTIL IT THICKENS. ONCE THE GRAVY IS READY, TAKE THE TURKEY WINGS FROM THE OVEN AND POUR THE GRAVY OVER THEM. RETURN THE WINGS TO THE OVEN UNCOVERED FOR 15 MORE MINUTES TO ENHANCE THE FLAVORS. FINALLY, TAKE THEM OUT OF THE OVEN AND SAVOR YOUR DELICIOUS CREATION!

124

SOUTHERN CHICKEN AND DRESSING

 Prep Time
20 minutes

 Cooking Time
50 Minutes

INGREDIENTS

4 cups crumbled corn bread

2 cups breadcrumbs

1 teaspoon creole seasoning

1 teaspoon garlic powder

1 teaspoon onion powder

1 teaspoon sage

1 teaspoon thyme

1 chicken bouillon packet

3 cups chopped chicken

1/3 cup butter

3 stalks celery chopped

3 stalks onion chopped

3 eggs

5 cups chicken stock or broth

DIRECTIONS 6

IN A LARGE BOWL, COMBINE THE BREADS, SEASONINGS, CHICKEN BOUILLON PACKET, AND CHICKEN, THEN SET IT ASIDE. IN A LARGE PAN OVER MEDIUM HEAT, MELT THE BUTTER AND SAUTÉ THE CELERY AND ONIONS UNTIL THEY ARE TENDER. ONCE COOKED, REMOVE FROM THE STOVE AND POUR THE MIXTURE INTO THE BOWL WITH THE BREAD AND CHICKEN. NEXT, ADD THE EGGS AND CHICKEN BROTH, MIXING THOROUGHLY. CONTINUE TO INCORPORATE MORE BROTH UNTIL THE MIXTURE REACHES A CONSISTENCY SIMILAR TO THICK SOUP (IT SHOULD BE QUITE SOUPY, AS IT WILL DRY OUT DURING COOKING). BAKE IN A GREASED BAKING DISH FOR APPROXIMATELY 50 MINUTES OR UNTIL IT TURNS A GOLDEN BROWN. NOW ENJOY.

★★★★☆

SOUTHERN POTATO SALAD

 Prep Time
15 Minutes

 Cooking Time
25 TO 30 MINUTES

INGREDIENTS

6 large potatoes cut into chunks

8 eggs chopped fine

1/2 medium onion

1 cup sweet pickles (or relish)

2 celery stalks (chopped fine)

1 1/2 cups mayonnaise

1 tablespoon mustard

1 tablespoon onion powder

1 tablespoon sugar

Salt and pepper to taste

DIRECTIONS   6

TO PREPARE THIS DELIGHTFUL POTATO SALAD, BEGIN BY BOILING THE POTATOES IN A LARGE POT SET TO MEDIUM HEAT UNTIL THEY ARE FORK-TENDER, WHICH SHOULD TAKE ABOUT 10 MINUTES. ONCE COOKED, REMOVE AND DRAIN THE POTATOES. IN A SEPARATE POT, PLACE THE EGGS AND COOK ON HIGH HEAT FOR 10 MINUTES. AFTERWARD, TURN OFF THE STOVE AND LET THE EGGS SIT FOR AN ADDITIONAL 10 MINUTES. COOL THE EGGS BY RUNNING COLD WATER OVER THEM, THEN PEEL AND CHOP THEM, SETTING THEM ASIDE.

IN A LARGE BOWL, COMBINE THE POTATOES, CHOPPED EGGS, ONIONS, SWEET PICKLES, CELERY, MAYONNAISE, MUSTARD, ONION POWDER, SUGAR, AND SALT AND PEPPER. STIR EVERYTHING TOGETHER THOROUGHLY, THEN SPRINKLE PAPRIKA ON TOP. REFRIGERATE THE SALAD TO SERVE IT COLD, OR ENJOY IT WARM. BON APPÉTIT!

SQUASH CASSEROLE

 Prep Time 25 minutes

 Cooking Time
45 to 50 Minutes

INGREDIENTS

JIFFY CORN BREAD

1 box Jiffy

1 Egg

1/3 cup milk

REGULAR CORN BREAD

2 cups corn meal

1 egg

½ cup milk

¼ cup water

1 tablespoon olive oil

THE FILLING

1 onion chopped

2 squashes chopped

2 zucchinis chopped

8 oz sharp cheddar

8 oz gouda cheese

1 stick butter

Salt and pepper to taste

1 teaspoon roasted garlic paste

1 tablespoon garlic powder

1 tablespoon onion powder

1 teaspoon celery seeds

1 ½ teaspoon sage

1 Goya chicken, bouillon

powder

3 eggs

2 ½ cups chicken broth

1 teaspoon smoked paprika.

🍴 6

DIRECTIONS

TO CREATE THIS DELECTABLE SQUASH CASSEROLE, BEGIN BY PREPARING A BATCH OF REGULAR CORNBREAD. IN A MEDIUM BOWL, COMBINE CORNMEAL, EGGS, BUTTERMILK, AND OIL, MIXING THOROUGHLY. POUR ABOUT A TABLESPOON OF OIL INTO A CAST-IRON PAN AND USE YOUR FINGERS TO SPREAD IT EVENLY ACROSS THE SURFACE. POUR THE BATTER INTO THE PAN, THEN BAKE IT IN A PREHEATED 350°F OVEN FOR 25 TO 30 MINUTES, UNTIL GOLDEN BROWN. ONCE DONE, REMOVE IT FROM THE OVEN AND ALLOW IT TO COOL.

NEXT, FOR THE JIFFY CORNBREAD, TAKE TWO PACKAGES OF JIFFY MUFFIN MIX, TWO EGGS, AND 2/3 CUP OF MILK, MIXING THEM TOGETHER IN A BOWL. COAT A MEDIUM CAST-IRON PAN WITH A TABLESPOON OF BUTTER, THEN POUR IN THE JIFFY BATTER. BAKE IN THE OVEN FOR 25 MINUTES UNTIL IT TURNS GOLDEN BROWN. AFTER BAKING, REMOVE IT FROM THE OVEN AND LET IT REST.

IN A LARGE BOWL, CRUMBLE BOTH CORNBREADS TOGETHER AND SET ASIDE. IN A LARGE SKILLET OVER MEDIUM HEAT, MELT SOME BUTTER AND ADD ZUCCHINI, SQUASH, AND ONIONS. SAUTÉ UNTIL TENDER, ABOUT 4 MINUTES, THEN TRANSFER THIS MIXTURE TO THE BOWL WITH THE CORNBREAD. INCORPORATE THE EGGS, CHICKEN STOCK, ALL SEASONINGS, 1 CUP OF CHEDDAR CHEESE, AND ALL THE GOUDA CHEESE, MIXING UNTIL COMBINED.

POUR THE MIXTURE INTO A BAKING DISH AND SPRINKLE THE REMAINING CHEDDAR CHEESE ON TOP. BAKE IN A 350°F OVEN FOR 45 MINUTES. TO CHECK FOR DONENESS, INSERT A TOOTHPICK INTO THE CENTER; IF IT COMES OUT CLEAN, IT'S READY. REMOVE FROM THE OVEN AND LET IT REST FOR 15 MINUTES BEFORE SERVING. ENJOY!

★★★★☆  9x13 Inch

ROASTED TURKEY

 Prep Time
20 minutes

 Cooking Time
50 Minutes

INGREDIENTS

Large Turkey,
giblets and neck
removed

24 oz honey gold baby
potatoes (sliced in half)

5 rainbow color carrots
(chopped)

4 stalks celery chopped

1 orange sliced

1 lemon sliced

1 whole onion chopped

1 ½ cup Toney's creole
Butter

1 whole bud of garlic
(top sliced off)

-Herb Butter-

¼ cup chopped
rosemary

¼ cup chopped thyme

¼ cup chopped parsley

1 tablespoon poultry
seasoning

1 tablespoon garlic
powder

1 tablespoon creole

1 teaspoon paprika

1 cup butter

1 ½ teaspoon salt

½ teaspoon pepper

Seasoning Blend

1 tablespoon creole
seasoning

1 tablespoon poultry
seasoning

1 tablespoon garlic
powder

DIRECTIONS 6

TO PREPARE THIS FLAVORFUL TURKEY, START BY USING A LARGE ROASTING PAN. PLACE THE POTATOES AND CARROTS AT THE BOTTOM, THEN ADD A RACK ON TOP OF THEM AND SET ASIDE. NEXT, CREATE THE HERB BUTTER. IN A MEDIUM BOWL, COMBINE ROSEMARY, THYME, PARSLEY, POULTRY SEASONING, GARLIC POWDER, CREOLE SEASONING, PAPRIKA, BUTTER, SALT, AND PEPPER, MIXING WELL UNTIL FULLY COMBINED. SET THIS MIXTURE ASIDE. AFTER CLEANING THE TURKEY, PAT IT DRY WITH A PAPER TOWEL TO HELP THE HERB BUTTER ADHERE EASILY. GENEROUSLY SPREAD THE HERB BUTTER UNDER THE TURKEY SKIN WHEREVER POSSIBLE, THEN APPLY IT TO THE OUTSIDE OF THE TURKEY AS WELL, ENSURING TO COVER THE BACK BY FLIPPING IT OVER. ONCE THIS IS COMPLETE, SET THE TURKEY ASIDE. IN A SMALL BOWL, MIX TOGETHER SOME POULTRY SEASONING, GARLIC POWDER, AND CREOLE SEASONING. SPRINKLE THIS MIXTURE ALL OVER THE TURKEY. PLACE THE TURKEY ON THE RACK ABOVE THE POTATOES AND CARROTS. NOW IT'S TIME TO INJECT THE TURKEY. USING TONY'S CREOLE BUTTER AND AN INJECTOR, INJECT THE TURKEY ALL OVER, FOCUSING ON THE LEGS, WINGS, AND ESPECIALLY THE BREAST, TO PREVENT IT FROM DRYING OUT. AFTER INJECTING, STUFF THE TURKEY WITH GARLIC, CELERY, ONIONS, ORANGES, AND LEMON. ONCE STUFFED, TIE IT UP USING COOKING TWINE, SECURING THE WINGS AND LEGS. COVER THE TIP OF THE TURKEY WITH FOIL, ENSURING IT DOESN'T TOUCH THE SKIN TO AVOID OVER-BROWNING. PREHEAT YOUR OVEN TO 375 DEGREES AND COOK THE TURKEY FOR ONE HOUR. AFTERWARD, REMOVE IT FROM THE OVEN AND BASTE IT. REPLACE THE FOIL AND RETURN IT TO THE OVEN FOR ANOTHER HOUR, REPEATING THE BASTING PROCESS UNTIL THE TURKEY IS FULLY COOKED. COOKING TIME WILL VARY BASED ON THE TURKEY'S WEIGHT. WHEN IT REACHES AN INTERNAL TEMPERATURE OF 165 DEGREES, IT IS DONE. REMOVE THE FOIL AND PLACE THE TURKEY BACK IN THE OVEN TO BROWN FOR AN ADDITIONAL 30 MINUTES OR UNTIL GOLDEN BROWN. FINALLY, TAKE IT OUT OF THE OVEN AND LET IT REST FOR 15 TO 20 MINUTES BEFORE SERVING.

TURNIP GREENS

 Prep Time
30 Minutes

 Cooking Time
3 Hours

INGREDIENTS

4 bunches of fresh turnip greens

1 pack of smoked turkey wings

(should be about 2 wings)

2 tablespoons olive oil

1 whole onion chopped

1 fresh garlic cloves chopped

4 cups chicken stock

1 cup water

1 serrano pepper chopped

1 tablespoon garlic powder

1 tablespoon onion powder

salt and pepper to taste

For Cleaning

1 teaspoon baking soda

1 tablespoon apple cider vinegar

Full bowl of Water

DIRECTIONS 6

TO PREPARE THESE DELICIOUS TURNIP GREENS, START BY GIVING THEM A THOROUGH TRIPLE WASH. I RECOMMEND USING APPLE CIDER VINEGAR AND BAKING SODA FOR THIS TASK. FILL TWO BOWLS WITH WATER MIXED WITH BAKING SODA AND VINEGAR, THEN WASH THE GREENS THREE TO FOUR TIMES UNTIL ALL GRIT AND SAND ARE REMOVED. BE SURE TO REFRESH THE BOWLS WITH CLEAN WATER, VINEGAR, AND BAKING SODA EACH TIME. ONCE THE GREENS ARE CLEAN, THEY ARE READY FOR COOKING.

IN A LARGE POT, HEAT OIL OVER MEDIUM HEAT AND ADD THE ONIONS. SAUTÉ THE ONIONS UNTIL THEY TURN TRANSLUCENT, WHICH SHOULD TAKE ABOUT TWO TO THREE MINUTES, THEN ADD THE GARLIC. COOK THE GARLIC FOR ANOTHER MINUTE BEFORE INTRODUCING THE TURNIP GREENS. POUR IN THE CHICKEN STOCK AND WATER, MAKING SURE NOT TO OVERFILL THE POT TO AVOID ANY SPILLS AS IT HEATS.

PLACE THE SMOKED TURKEY ON TOP OF THE GREENS AND COVER THE POT WITH A LID. LET IT SIMMER FOR ONE HOUR, THEN ADD THE CHOPPED SERRANO PEPPERS, GARLIC POWDER, AND ONION POWDER, MIXING EVERYTHING WELL BEFORE COVERING THE POT AGAIN. CHECK ON THE POT EVERY HOUR TO ENSURE THE SMOKED TURKEY BECOMES TENDER AND EASILY FALLS OFF THE BONE— THIS SHOULD HAPPEN AFTER ABOUT THREE HOURS. ONCE THE MEAT HAS FALLEN OFF THE BONE, REMOVE THE BONES FROM THE TURNIP GREENS AND DISCARD THEM.

YOUR GREENS ARE NOW READY! JUST SEASON WITH SALT AND PEPPER, AND DON'T FORGET TO SERVE WITH CORNBREAD. ENJOY!

MEAL PLANNING

WEEKLY PLANS

Sun		
Mon		
Tue		
Wed		
Thu		
Fri		
Sat		

PLAN FOR THE WEEK

meal planner

WEEK OF: _____   MONTH: _____

MONDAY	BREAKFAST	
	LUNCH	
	DINNER	
TUESDAY	BREAKFAST	
	LUNCH	
	DINNER	
WEDNESDAY	BREAKFAST	
	LUNCH	
	DINNER	
THURSDAY	BREAKFAST	
	LUNCH	
	DINNER	
FRIDAY	BREAKFAST	
	LUNCH	
	DINNER	
SATURDAY	BREAKFAST	
	LUNCH	
	DINNER	
SUNDAY	BREAKFAST	
	LUNCH	
	DINNER	

GROCERY LIST
◇ _____
◇ _____
◇ _____
◇ _____
◇ _____
◇ _____
◇ _____
◇ _____
◇ _____

SNACKS

NOTES
_____
_____
_____

132

meal planner

WEEK OF: MONTH:

MONDAY	BREAKFAST
	LUNCH
	DINNER
TUESDAY	BREAKFAST
	LUNCH
	DINNER
WEDNESDAY	BREAKFAST
	LUNCH
	DINNER
THURSDAY	BREAKFAST
	LUNCH
	DINNER
FRIDAY	BREAKFAST
	LUNCH
	DINNER
SATURDAY	BREAKFAST
	LUNCH
	DINNER
SUNDAY	BREAKFAST
	LUNCH
	DINNER

GROCERY LIST

◇ _____
◇ _____
◇ _____
◇ _____
◇ _____
◇ _____
◇ _____
◇ _____
◇ _____
◇ _____

SNACKS

NOTES

_____
_____
_____

meal planner

WEEK OF: MONTH:

MONDAY	BREAKFAST	
	LUNCH	
	DINNER	
TUESDAY	BREAKFAST	
	LUNCH	
	DINNER	
WEDNESDAY	BREAKFAST	
	LUNCH	
	DINNER	
THURSDAY	BREAKFAST	
	LUNCH	
	DINNER	
FRIDAY	BREAKFAST	
	LUNCH	
	DINNER	
SATURDAY	BREAKFAST	
	LUNCH	
	DINNER	
SUNDAY	BREAKFAST	
	LUNCH	
	DINNER	

GROCERY LIST

◇ _____
◇ _____
◇ _____
◇ _____
◇ _____
◇ _____
◇ _____
◇ _____
◇ _____

SNACKS

NOTES

_____
_____
_____

134

meal planner

WEEK OF: MONTH:

MONDAY	BREAKFAST	
	LUNCH	
	DINNER	
TUESDAY	BREAKFAST	
	LUNCH	
	DINNER	
WEDNESDAY	BREAKFAST	
	LUNCH	
	DINNER	
THURSDAY	BREAKFAST	
	LUNCH	
	DINNER	
FRIDAY	BREAKFAST	
	LUNCH	
	DINNER	
SATURDAY	BREAKFAST	
	LUNCH	
	DINNER	
SUNDAY	BREAKFAST	
	LUNCH	
	DINNER	

GROCERY LIST

◇ _____
◇ _____
◇ _____
◇ _____
◇ _____
◇ _____
◇ _____
◇ _____
◇ _____
◇ _____

SNACKS

NOTES

_____
_____
_____

meal planner

WEEK OF: _____   MONTH: _____

MONDAY	BREAKFAST	
	LUNCH	
	DINNER	
TUESDAY	BREAKFAST	
	LUNCH	
	DINNER	
WEDNESDAY	BREAKFAST	
	LUNCH	
	DINNER	
THURSDAY	BREAKFAST	
	LUNCH	
	DINNER	
FRIDAY	BREAKFAST	
	LUNCH	
	DINNER	
SATURDAY	BREAKFAST	
	LUNCH	
	DINNER	
SUNDAY	BREAKFAST	
	LUNCH	
	DINNER	

GROCERY LIST

◇ _____
◇ _____
◇ _____
◇ _____
◇ _____
◇ _____
◇ _____
◇ _____
◇ _____
◇ _____

SNACKS

NOTES

_____
_____
_____

meal planner

WEEK OF: **MONTH:**

MONDAY	BREAKFAST	
	LUNCH	
	DINNER	
TUESDAY	BREAKFAST	
	LUNCH	
	DINNER	
WEDNESDAY	BREAKFAST	
	LUNCH	
	DINNER	
THURSDAY	BREAKFAST	
	LUNCH	
	DINNER	
FRIDAY	BREAKFAST	
	LUNCH	
	DINNER	
SATURDAY	BREAKFAST	
	LUNCH	
	DINNER	
SUNDAY	BREAKFAST	
	LUNCH	
	DINNER	

GROCERY LIST

◇ _____
◇ _____
◇ _____
◇ _____
◇ _____
◇ _____
◇ _____
◇ _____
◇ _____

SNACKS

NOTES

_____
_____
_____

meal planner

WEEK OF: MONTH:

MONDAY	BREAKFAST	
	LUNCH	
	DINNER	
TUESDAY	BREAKFAST	
	LUNCH	
	DINNER	
WEDNESDAY	BREAKFAST	
	LUNCH	
	DINNER	
THURSDAY	BREAKFAST	
	LUNCH	
	DINNER	
FRIDAY	BREAKFAST	
	LUNCH	
	DINNER	
SATURDAY	BREAKFAST	
	LUNCH	
	DINNER	
SUNDAY	BREAKFAST	
	LUNCH	
	DINNER	

GROCERY LIST

◇ _____
◇ _____
◇ _____
◇ _____
◇ _____
◇ _____
◇ _____
◇ _____
◇ _____

SNACKS

NOTES

_____
_____
_____

138

meal planner

WEEK OF: MONTH:

MONDAY	BREAKFAST	
	LUNCH	
	DINNER	
TUESDAY	BREAKFAST	
	LUNCH	
	DINNER	
WEDNESDAY	BREAKFAST	
	LUNCH	
	DINNER	
THURSDAY	BREAKFAST	
	LUNCH	
	DINNER	
FRIDAY	BREAKFAST	
	LUNCH	
	DINNER	
SATURDAY	BREAKFAST	
	LUNCH	
	DINNER	
SUNDAY	BREAKFAST	
	LUNCH	
	DINNER	

GROCERY LIST

◇ _____
◇ _____
◇ _____
◇ _____
◇ _____
◇ _____
◇ _____
◇ _____
◇ _____

SNACKS

NOTES

_____
_____
_____

meal planner

WEEK OF: MONTH:

MONDAY	BREAKFAST	
	LUNCH	
	DINNER	
TUESDAY	BREAKFAST	
	LUNCH	
	DINNER	
WEDNESDAY	BREAKFAST	
	LUNCH	
	DINNER	
THURSDAY	BREAKFAST	
	LUNCH	
	DINNER	
FRIDAY	BREAKFAST	
	LUNCH	
	DINNER	
SATURDAY	BREAKFAST	
	LUNCH	
	DINNER	
SUNDAY	BREAKFAST	
	LUNCH	
	DINNER	

GROCERY LIST

◇ _____
◇ _____
◇ _____
◇ _____
◇ _____
◇ _____
◇ _____
◇ _____
◇ _____
◇ _____

SNACKS

NOTES

_____
_____
_____

meal planner

WEEK OF: MONTH:

MONDAY	BREAKFAST	
	LUNCH	
	DINNER	
TUESDAY	BREAKFAST	
	LUNCH	
	DINNER	
WEDNESDAY	BREAKFAST	
	LUNCH	
	DINNER	
THURSDAY	BREAKFAST	
	LUNCH	
	DINNER	
FRIDAY	BREAKFAST	
	LUNCH	
	DINNER	
SATURDAY	BREAKFAST	
	LUNCH	
	DINNER	
SUNDAY	BREAKFAST	
	LUNCH	
	DINNER	

GROCERY LIST

◇ _____
◇ _____
◇ _____
◇ _____
◇ _____
◇ _____
◇ _____
◇ _____
◇ _____
◇ _____

SNACKS

NOTES

_____
_____
_____

141

meal planner

WEEK OF: MONTH:

MONDAY	BREAKFAST	
	LUNCH	
	DINNER	
TUESDAY	BREAKFAST	
	LUNCH	
	DINNER	
WEDNESDAY	BREAKFAST	
	LUNCH	
	DINNER	
THURSDAY	BREAKFAST	
	LUNCH	
	DINNER	
FRIDAY	BREAKFAST	
	LUNCH	
	DINNER	
SATURDAY	BREAKFAST	
	LUNCH	
	DINNER	
SUNDAY	BREAKFAST	
	LUNCH	
	DINNER	

GROCERY LIST

◇ _____
◇ _____
◇ _____
◇ _____
◇ _____
◇ _____
◇ _____
◇ _____
◇ _____
◇ _____

SNACKS

NOTES

_____
_____
_____

RECIPE CARDS

YOUR RECIPES

COOKING WITH LOVE

recipe card

○ ○ ○ ○ ○
DIFFICULTY

NAME OF DISH

CATEGORY

PREP TIME

COOK TIME

INGREDIENTS

directions

- ....
- ....
- ....
- ....
- ....
- ....
- ....
- ....
- ....
- ....
- ....

....
....
....
....
....
....
....
....
....
....
....

notes

....
....
....
....
....

recipe card

○ ○ ○ ○ ○
DIFFICULTY

NAME OF DISH

CATEGORY

PREP TIME

COOK TIME

INGREDIENTS

- ....
- ....
- ....
- ....
- ....
- ....
- ....
- ....
- ....
- ....

directions

....
....
....
....
....
....
....
....
....
....
....
....
....
....

notes

recipe card

○ ○ ○ ○ ○
DIFFICULTY

NAME OF DISH

CATEGORY   PREP TIME   COOK TIME

INGREDIENTS   *directions*

- ....
- ....
- ....
- ....
- ....
- ....
- ....
- ....
- ....
- ....
- ....

notes

recipe card

○ ○ ○ ○ ○
DIFFICULTY

NAME OF DISH

CATEGORY

PREP TIME

COOK TIME

INGREDIENTS

- ....
- ....
- ....
- ....
- ....
- ....
- ....
- ....
- ....
- ....
- ....

directions

....

....

....

....

....

....

....

....

....

....

....

....

....

....

....

....

notes

recipe card

○ ○ ○ ○ ○
DIFFICULTY

NAME OF DISH

CATEGORY

PREP TIME

COOK TIME

_____

_____

_____

INGREDIENTS

- ....
- ....
- ....
- ....
- ....
- ....
- ....
- ....
- ....
- ....
- ....

directions

....

....

....

....

....

....

....

....

....

....

....

notes

....

....

....

....

recipe card

○ ○ ○ ○ ○
DIFFICULTY

NAME OF DISH

CATEGORY

PREP TIME

COOK TIME

INGREDIENTS

- ....
- ....
- ....
- ....
- ....
- ....
- ....
- ....
- ....
- ....

directions

....
....
....
....
....
....
....
....
....
....
....
....
....
....
....

notes

recipe card

○ ○ ○ ○ ○
DIFFICULTY

NAME OF DISH

CATEGORY

PREP TIME

COOK TIME

INGREDIENTS

- ....
- ....
- ....
- ....
- ....
- ....
- ....
- ....
- ....
- ....
- ....

directions

....
....
....
....
....
....
....
....
....
....
....
....
....
....
....
....

notes

recipe card

○ ○ ○ ○ ○
DIFFICULTY

NAME OF DISH

CATEGORY

PREP TIME

COOK TIME

INGREDIENTS

- ....
- ....
- ....
- ....
- ....
- ....
- ....
- ....
- ....
- ....
- ....

directions

....
....
....
....
....
....
....
....
....
....
....
....
....
....
....

notes

recipe card

○ ○ ○ ○ ○
DIFFICULTY

NAME OF DISH

CATEGORY   PREP TIME   COOK TIME

_____   _____   _____

INGREDIENTS

- ....
- ....
- ....
- ....
- ....
- ....
- ....
- ....
- ....
- ....
- ....

directions

....
....
....
....
....
....
....
....
....
....
....
....
....
....
....

notes

recipe card

○ ○ ○ ○ ○
DIFFICULTY

NAME OF DISH

CATEGORY

PREP TIME

COOK TIME

INGREDIENTS

- ....
- ....
- ....
- ....
- ....
- ....
- ....
- ....
- ....
- ....
- ....

directions

....
....
....
....
....
....
....
....
....
....
....
....
....
....
....

notes

recipe card

○ ○ ○ ○ ○
DIFFICULTY

NAME OF DISH

CATEGORY
_____

PREP TIME
_____

COOK TIME
_____

INGREDIENTS

- ....
- ....
- ....
- ....
- ....
- ....
- ....
- ....
- ....
- ....

directions

....
....
....
....
....
....
....
....
....
....
....
....
....
....
....

notes

A Heartfelt Appreciation:

I want to express my deepest gratitude to my husband, Josh Harris, who consistently supports me no matter how wild my ideas may be. Thank you for believing in me, encouraging me to persevere, and praying for me, our family, and our dreams. Your unwavering love, strength as the family's provider, and your role as the household leader are truly appreciated. I am grateful for your unconditional love and your steadfast faith. You are a remarkable man of God, and I love you immensely.

To my daughter Kokeeta Calhoun,

You are my true inspiration. Every day, I see someone who has overcome the seemingly impossible. Your challenges put mine into perspective, yet you handle them effortlessly. God has blessed you with a unique spirit – one of compassion, support, generosity, forgiveness, and love. I am thankful that He entrusted me to be your mother. My love for you is beyond measure. Thank you! ♥

To my sons Kadeem and Joshua,

I want to take a moment to express just how thankful I am for your unwavering support. Your encouragement and love have been a constant source of strength for me. Watching you grow and achieve your goals fills my heart with immense pride. Each of your accomplishments, big or small, is a testament to your hard work, dedication, and the wonderful individuals you have become. I am so grateful to have you in my life. Your support means the world to me, and I am incredibly proud to be your mom.

I love you both with every part of me. Seeing the amazing people you are becoming fills me with joy and gratitude. You inspire me every day with your kindness, determination, and resilience. I am proud of the men you are growing into and the values you uphold. Being your mom is the greatest blessing, and I am thankful for the bond we share. Always remember that I am here for you, cheering you on every step of the way. I love you more than words can express, and I am so proud to call you my sons.

My dear sister Kim,

I want to take a moment to express just how grateful and blessed I feel to have you in my life. Your unwavering support and love have been a constant source of strength for me. Whether it's been through the highs or the lows, you've always been there, offering a listening ear, a comforting hug, and words of wisdom. I truly cherish the bond we share and the countless memories we've created together. Your kindness, generosity, and understanding mean the world to me, and I am so thankful to have you as my sister.

Thank you for always believing in me and supporting me on my journey. Your encouragement has given me the confidence to pursue my dreams and face challenges head-on. Knowing that I have you by my side makes everything seem possible. I am deeply appreciative of all the sacrifices you've made and the love you've shown. You are not just my sister, but my best friend and my biggest cheerleader. I am forever grateful for you and the incredible person you are.

A LITTLE INSPIRATION

Having faith and following your dreams is a powerful combination that can lead to the manifestation of your heart's deepest desires. Faith is the foundation that gives you the strength to pursue your dreams, even when the path seems uncertain. It's about believing in yourself and the possibilities that lie ahead. When you have faith, you can overcome obstacles and stay focused on your goals. Writing down your prayers and dreams is a crucial step in this journey. The power is in the pen; by putting your thoughts and aspirations on paper, you are setting your intentions and making a commitment to yourself. This act of writing helps to clarify your vision and keeps you motivated to achieve it.

However, faith without works is dead. It's not enough to simply believe; you must also take action towards your dreams. Walking in your destiny requires effort, perseverance, and a proactive approach. You need to work diligently, make plans, and take steps that align with your goals. Be grateful for every opportunity and challenge that comes your way, as they are all part of your journey. Gratitude keeps you grounded and reminds you of the progress you've made. Embrace your path with an open heart and a determined spirit, knowing that with faith, hard work, and a grateful mindset, you can manifest the life you desire.

CLOSING

As we come to the end of this cookbook, I want to extend my heartfelt gratitude to you for joining me on this culinary journey. Each recipe in these pages is a labor of love, crafted with the hope of bringing joy and deliciousness to your kitchen. Cooking is more than just preparing food; it's about creating memories, sharing moments, and expressing love through every dish. I hope these recipes inspire you to experiment, savor new flavors, and most importantly, enjoy the process of cooking. Remember, the kitchen is a place where magic happens, and every meal is an opportunity to create something special.

Thank you for allowing me to be a part of your cooking adventures. I am honored to share these recipes with you and hope they become cherished favorites in your home. As you continue to explore and create, may you find joy in every bite and satisfaction in every meal. Cooking is a journey, and I am grateful to have been a part of yours. Here's to many more delicious moments and happy memories in the kitchen. I guess I will see you on the next one...

Bye Now - Kellz

INDEX OF RECIPES

INDEX OF RECIPES

Made in the USA
Columbia, SC
20 November 2024

46199aec-fe03-4eb4-bd37-5356b0f01d78R01